Contents

PR IN PRACTICE SERIES

Public Relations Strategy

Sandra Oliver

the Institute *of* Public Relations

**KOGAN
PAGE**

659.2

With acknowledgement to the International Public Relations Association and the companies concerned for their kind permission to include a selection of winning Golden World Award programmes.

First published in 2001

Kogan Page Limited
120 Pentonville Road
London N1 9JN
UK

Kogan Page US
22 Broad Street
Milford CT 06460
USA

British Library Cataloguing in Publication Data

A CIP record for this book is available from the British Library.

ISBN 0 7494 3541 0

Typeset by Jean Cussons Typesetting, Diss, Norfolk
Printed and bound in Great Britain by Biddles Ltd, Guildford and King's Lynn

Foreword

As public relations has matured as a discipline, scholars and practitioners have come to recognize its strategic role. Not only is it strategic in itself – the management of relationships between an organization and all its stakeholders – but it also has a key communication role within other management operations.

This book is aimed at public relation practitioners who already have some organizational experience. Its intention is to help practitioners consider public relations from a business perspective. In doing this, it looks not only at practitioner considerations of tools and techniques, but also introduces relevant elements of management theory from the various disciplines that underpin them.

The book falls naturally into six key areas. In Chapter 1, there is a discussion of strategy itself. While most people at a senior level in organizations would regard their function as 'strategic', Sandra Oliver takes us back to a consideration of the nature of strategy and why public relations is a strategic discipline.

In Chapter 2, she expands on the specific role of public relations within organizations, and what it adds when practised at a strategic level.

A discussion about image and identity follows in Chapter 3. In an age where 'spin' appears to have reached its apotheosis, Sandra

Oliver provides us with a useful summary of how organizations obtain and maintain their reputations, and how substance must underpin all public relations activity.

Turning then to the human resource (HR) dimension, Chapter 4 looks at issues of internal communication, the communication responsibility of leaders and the assistance that public relations can offer to the HR discipline.

Within academic and practitioner circles there is constant debate about whether marketing is a subset of public relations or vice versa. In Chapter 5 Sandra Oliver looks at this relationship. She points out the scope of each discipline and how they overlap and interact. Her cogent considerations suggest that each discipline has a value in its own right and that each can bring useful insights and approaches to the other.

In Chapter 6, Sandra looks at public relations within the new media and Internet environment. She discusses how the nature of communication is changing and how the various communication disciplines are converging. She provides some useful indicators as to the role of public relations in the future.

This book, which is laced with substantive case studies to back up the points being made, is a most useful addition to the thinking practitioner's library. It will be particularly appropriate to those wishing to consider their discipline in a more strategic light. As such, it will provide a valuable source of information for those undertaking higher undergraduate, postgraduate and professional examinations in public relations and related disciplines, and to those senior practitioners who are constructing their own Continuing Professional Development scheme along the lines of the IPR's 'Developing Excellence' programme.

Strategic Public Relations is not a 'light read'. It requires the reader to engage in serious intellectual consideration of public relations, and to reflect at a profound level on its implications for their own practice. This practice will be all the better for having been challenged, critically analysed and, if necessary, reconstructed to be genuinely strategic.

Anne Gregory
Series Editor

Preface

This book offers a glimpse into the proliferation of theories and models that have emerged around strategic management in the last few years of e-commerce and the Internet. Global expansion for industry and commerce has not only brought public relations management into sharp focus again but is clarifying context and position in relation to other corporate priorities.

At the practical level, most in-house specialists are aware that they can carry out the tactical requirements demanded of them such as media relations, trade shows and publicity events, internal and external publication production, including video, audio and film production, the annual report and other activities. Yet many struggle with their main board directorate who, singly or collectively, ask questions which need a knowledge and appreciation of business strategy, let alone PR or communication strategy, before appropriate responses can be given.

Nature vs nurture

There is currently a fairly intense discussion taking place about the nature of strategic public relations, and this book emerged from a series of lively dialogues. Brainstorming inevitably produces moments of truth and this in turn provides raw material for the development of any body of knowledge. All subjects have a strategic element to them, and public relations is no exception. Like management, it is art rather than science, but of one thing we can be certain: e-commerce has changed not only the nature of public relations theory and practice, but also the nurturing necessary for the next generation of professional managers, whether in-house or in consultancy.

The public relations industry is at a juncture of development where there is much confusion about the context and boundaries of this discipline. While the subject of public relations is generally understood to be a management discipline, many university departments around the world choose either not to identify with it at all or to relegate it to being a subset of marketing, film or media studies departments. Of course, higher education generally is having to adapt to the information age and the complexities that this brings in all such interdisciplinary and multidisciplinary subjects, so to some extent the 'knowledge era' offers opportunities for public relations subject development not seen before. However, one issue that taxes the minds of academics is that of comparability to other 'accepted' disciplines.

Universities establish clear pathways with prescribed indicators to measure attainment of education (knowledge) and training (skill) at each stage of the process until specified learning outcomes are demonstrably achieved and an award given. In the acquisition of general management competencies, it is understood that students must have proven conceptual and tactical understanding of their subject at functional or operational level.

Within the practitioner community there is debate too, with one persuasion promoting the practical, tactical elements of the profession while another espouses approaches grounded in management thinking. A third school combines elements of both.

How far techniques might be included in this book on strategic management has raised some interesting academic dilemmas.

As a book claiming to represent the subject of public relations at the strategic level, it ought, by definition, to be able to assume that functional or operational mechanisms are understood and need not be reiterated. Students of public relations, for example, proceed from the IPR Foundation Diploma level before attempting the IPR Diploma, some of which concentrates on public relations strategy, while numerous practitioners, who may have years of professional, technical expertise behind them, approach strategic public relations with some trepidation when it comes to putting it into a theoretical, business context.

A compromise has therefore been reached whereby the reader can reflect and assess tactics through discussion of case examples provided at the end of each chapter. Thus the book begins by introducing readers to a variety of definitions of public relations before advancing towards higher-order aspects of strategic public relations from a managerial perspective within a business context.

Acknowledgements

My thanks to all my peers for the ever-stimulating and rigorous discourse that took place by phone, e-mail and at conferences around the globe during the writing of this book; to all the researchers cited in the text; and to practitioners and students at whatever stage of lifelong learning they happen to be, for their deeply valued interest and ongoing involvement.

Special mention must also go to the companies featured; the IPRA Golden World Award judging panel for their permission to include previous winning entries; and to IPR Education and the CPD subcommittee for comments during the development of its qualifying diploma and the formation of this Kogan Page/IPR 'PR in Practice' series.

1

Not 'just' PR: public relations strategy in a management context

FROM FUNCTION TO STRATEGY

When the Institute of Public Relations produced the results of their Delphi Survey in 1994, the need for definition of the term 'public relations' (PR) was second to the measurement and evaluation of public relations in a hierarchy of research requirements as articulated by Institute members, both academic and practitioner. With any developing profession, reliable and valid research brings it to maturity. However, if definition is still a problem, theories, models, techniques and strategies remain abstract concepts. Or do they? Who can clearly define all types of accountancy or law in a single definitive statement?

Many organizations, though, are making a move away from the term public relations towards the term communication management in the naming of their restructured public relations and public affairs departments. Like the term management, public relations may rely more for its meaning when things go wrong than when things go right! Practitioners are well aware of the function of public relations and the techniques applied in order to carry out its role in a business context. This chapter demonstrates how strategic public relations contributes to corporate business strategy by involving its full range of stakeholders. Before addressing this aspect, it is necessary to define what is meant by strategy.

WHAT IS STRATEGY?

J L Thompson (1995) defines strategy as a means to an end: 'The ends concern the purposes and objectives of the organization. There is a broad strategy for the whole organization and a competitive strategy for each activity. Functional strategies contribute directly to competitive strategies.' Bennett (1996) describes strategy as 'the direction that the organization chooses to follow in order to fulfil its mission'. Mintzberg offers five uses of the word strategy, namely:

- a plan – a consciously intended course of action;
- a ploy – a specific manoeuvre intended to outwit an opponent or competitors;
- a pattern – in a stream of actions;
- a position – a means of locating an organization in an environment;
- a perspective – an integrated way of perceiving the world.

He sees links between his five uses and makes the point throughout his writings that it is essential that his readers explore the different perspectives of an organization and its activities that each use gives. The reflective in-house public relations practitioner does this in the normal course of his or her professional control activity and will be aware that:

- Major public relations decisions affect or influence organizational objectives in the next few years;
- Public relations decisions involve a major commitment of resources;

- Public relations decisions involve complex situations at corporate, business unit or other stakeholder levels which may affect or be affected by many parts of the organization.

Throughout this book the following definitions based on a range of terms used by general management teachers and practitioners will be used:

- *Vision* – a written concept based on a function (task) or view (idea) of the organization.
- *Mission* – the fundamental purpose of an organization which underpins its strategy.
- *Strategy* – the means or process by which an organization aims to fulfil its mission.
- *Policy* – the formal and informal ground rules or criteria applied during decision making.
- *Objective* – a bottom-line, measurable statement of what must be achieved, often seen to be longer term than 'goal'.
- *Goal* – a concrete objective often seen to be shorter term.
- *Aim* – a combination of objective and goal, maybe both short and long term, sometimes involving hope and aspiration.
- *Tactic* – decisions and actions intended to achieve short-term objectives.

Although it differs from organization to organization, it is common practice for strategy making to take place at three levels, the corporate, the business unit and the operational level, although in small companies the business unit is often the corporate level, whereas in the Health Service for example, strategic decisions are made from central government downwards.

Communication strategies between various levels in organizations have to be consistent. There is often a lack of recognition of strategic decisions being made at different levels so the role of the public relations specialist is to ensure that consistency applies throughout, what the British politician Peter Mandelson referred to as being 'on message'. This did not mean 'common' or 'the same', although perception of the phrase was consistently changed by journalists and ministerial rivals to suggest that it did mean that.

THE NETWORK TRIANGLE

This book will focus on three main areas of public relations strategy: 1) business communication strategy, which includes public or government affairs and corporate reputation; 2) internal or human resource strategy, involving employees, managers, directors and shareholders; and 3) integrated marketing communication strategy. These three areas have come to be accepted as the three main research-based and supported dimensions of public relations, both in Europe and the United States, at this stage of its history. The importance of this to practitioners cannot be overestimated, given the critical role of monitoring and evaluation of campaign policy and planning.

The book also examines public relations within a multimedia, new technology context, a dimension that cannot be ignored in the 21st century.

AUDIENCES

The Institute of Public Relations' (IPR) definition of public relations was, until the mid-1980s, 'the planned and sustained effort to establish and maintain goodwill and mutual understanding between an organization and its publics'. Here, the definition implies strategic management by the inclusion of the words 'planned', 'sustained' and the use of the word 'publics' as plural.

Other definitions also clearly identify a strategic role for public relations, and the indicators are highlighted:

> Public relations is the management of **all communications** within the organization and between the organization and its outside audiences. The purpose is to create better understanding of the organization among its **audiences**.

and

> Public relations is the management of **all relationships** which are important to an organization. Circumstances will determine which **audiences or sub-audiences** are most important and need priority attention at any time.

Public relations is the management of the organization's reputation. It identifies the **perceptions** which are held of the organization and works to inform **all relevant audiences** about organization performance. It is concerned with developing a **deserved reputation** for an organization, one which is based on performance. This reputation will not necessarily be favourable, but only as favourable as the organization deserves.

KEY GROUPS

The IPR suggests that there are eight basic publics or key stakeholder groups in public relations which need to be serviced using all the tools and techniques available to the communication strategist to aid mutual understanding:

1. the community at large or people living near or affected by the organization's premises or practices;
2. employees, managers and their unions;
3. customers – past, present and future;
4. suppliers of materials and non-financial services;
5. the money market, including shareholders, banks, insurers and investors;
6. distributors, agents, wholesalers and retailers;
7. potential employees, consultants and agents;
8. opinion leaders, particularly radio, television, press and other media professionals or activists, including lobbyists and environmental pressure groups.

The role of public opinion in the activities of organizations continues to increase with the Internet and the public relations profession has always been aware of its obligations for ethical relations with all stakeholder groups. Edward Bernays said in 1923 that 'it is in the creation of a public conscience that the counsel on public relations is destined, I believe, to fulfil its highest usefulness to the society in which we live'. The Institute of Public Relations today endorses this thinking, nearly 80 years later, in its code of conduct.

INTEGRATING COMMUNICATION

Public relations strategy cannot be considered here without focusing on the concept and importance of integrated communication. It has already been stated that communicating consistently does not mean communicating the same message but, clearly, a fundamental requirement in public relations is to develop a consistent corporate message and tone that appropriately reflect the organization in the way that the organization wishes it to be reflected, even as events, crises and issues are occurring. At the same time, messages must be capable of being adapted creatively to be understood by the different audiences targeted. Nicholas Ind (1997) says, 'Communication strategies should always start from the need to be specifically and ideally quantifiable communication objectives. The over-arching goal should be to achieve a specific positioning that will transcend the objectives for different audiences. The positioning itself should be derived from analysis.' Ind also suggests that public relations functions are to increase awareness and improve favourability. 'Public relations loses out to advertising in its controllability, but it has the advantage over advertising in its ability to communicate more complex messages and in its credibility. The press coverage achieved through media relations activity has the appearance of neutrality. Also the ability to target specific media and audiences is enhanced by the flexibility public relations offers (1997: 80).

This requires that a public relations strategy has to consider the ways that all its activities can be integrated and the most practical and definitive way currently is to base public relations programmes on audience or stakeholder analysis. Just as it is critical to understand the theory and practice of customer relations in order to sell anything, so it is critical to understand what the different audiences or stakeholders need to know, where they are coming from in response to a message or organization's reputation, so that the principles of mutual understanding, not necessarily agreement, can be applied. As Ind says, 'a communications strategy can then be evolved which specifies within an overall positioning the communication requirements for each specific audience. This should not encourage communication anarchy with messages to shareholders contradicting those to consumers, but relevance. Working from audiences inwards encourages an organization to think of its communication mechanisms appropriately.'

SEMANTICS

While the public relations industry owes a debt of gratitude to the marketing industry for its development of research tools, the fact that much quantitative and qualitative data has emerged from the discipline of marketing has led to some of the semantic confusion of the last decade referred to earlier. For example, one group of marketers defined public relations as 'building good relations with the company's various publics by obtaining favourable publicity, building up a good corporate image and handling or heading off unfavourable rumours, stories and events'. These academic marketers (Kotler *et al*, 1999) view public relations as a mass promotion technique and suggest that the old name for marketing public relations was publicity which was 'seen simply as activities to promote a company or its products by planting news about it in media not paid for by the sponsor'. Acknowledging that public relations goes beyond the customer public or audience, they concur with the public relations industry that some of the tools or techniques include media relations, press relations, product publicity, lobbying and counselling.

From a strategic point of view this subjugates the function of public relations to the marketing strategy and, although marketing strategy may be linked to corporate business strategy, it fails to address the direct links of public relations to corporate strategy. Strategy is regarded as longer-term planning while the tactics used are more often short term in effect, although of course either can impact on strategic decision making in changing circumstances. Public relations is concerned with managing the relationships between an organization and a wide variety of publics or audiences. The development of macroeconomics and environmental management studies has put pressure on the public relations industry to focus public relations strategy on the dimension of the enterprise or organization which goes beyond the bottom line of profit and includes measures of success based on social accountability. As well as an organization's role in the economic life of its country and its position in the global or national marketplace, public relations counsel and activities form an important part of an organization's policy in defining the environmental factors which affect its corporate business activities. These include social stratification, social welfare and national policy, technology, and the political, legal and regulatory processes appropriate to a particular organization or the industry in which it operates.

PUBLIC RELATIONS PRACTICE

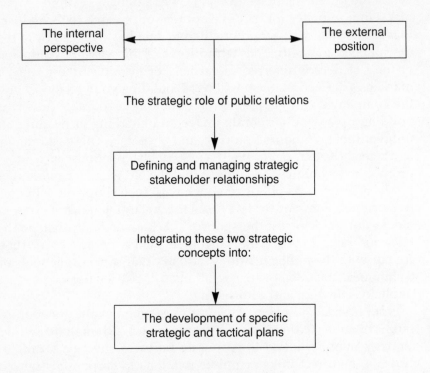

Figure 1.1 *The strategic role of public relations*

The classical models of strategic management try to balance the internal and external perspectives by correlating corporate mission with external environmental factors over time. The steps a strategic manager would take in monitoring this exercise might be as follows:

1. Determination of the *mission* of the company, including broad statements.
2. Development of a company *profile* that reflects its internal condition and capability.
3. Assessment of the company's *external environment*, in terms of both competitive and general contextual factors.
4. *Interactive opportunity analysis* of possible options uncovered in the matching of the company profile with the external environment.

5. *Identification of desired options* uncovered when the set of possibilities is considered in light of the company mission.
6. Strategic choice of a set of long-term objectives and *grand strategies* needed to achieve the desired options.
7. Development of annual *objectives* and short-term strategies that are compatible with the long-term objectives and grand strategies.
8. *Implementation* of strategic choice decisions using budgeted resources and matching tasks, people, structures, technologies and reward systems.
9. Review and *evaluation* of the success of the strategic process to serve as a basis of control and as an input for future decision making.

Source: Pearce and Robinson (1982) cited in Grunig (1992)

Inevitably, a crucial factor in this exercise is relations with the media and identifying the nature of the desired communications as indicated by Grunig and Hunt's summary in Table 1.1.

Grunig *et al* (1992) identified half of American companies as using the public information model, 20 per cent using the two-way asymmetric model and only 15 per cent using one or other of the press agentry/publicity model or the two-way symmetric model. Of course, no one model is mutually exclusive and all four models may be applied within a single programme, obviously not necessarily simultaneously but as appropriate for specific requirements. Grunig and his researchers at the IABC asserted that quality assurance can only be achieved through the two-way symmetrical model, which relies heavily on the quality management of feedback.

FEEDBACK

Given the close psychological connection between perception and communication, critical feedback data will include identifying the responses to a message from receivers. The traditional emphasis on feedback as knowledge and intelligence is as important as ever, but is changing in scale as a result of computer-assisted software.

Table 1.1 *Four public relations models*

Characteristic	Model			
	Press agentry/ publicity	*Public information*	*Two-way asymmetric*	*Two-way symmetric*
Purpose	Propaganda	Dissemination of information	Scientific persuasion	Mutual understanding
Nature of communication	One-way; complete truth not essential	One-way; truth important	Two-way; imbalanced effects	Two-way; balanced effects
Communication model	Source → Rec.	Source → Rec.	Source → Rec. ↓ Feedback	Group → Group ↓
Nature of research	Little; 'counting house'	Little; readability, readership	Formative; evaluative of attitudes	Formative; evaluative of understanding
Leading historical figures	P T Barnum	Ivy Lee	Edward L Bernays	Bernays, educators, professional leaders
Where practised today	Sports, theatre, product promotion	Government, nonprofit associations, business	Competitive business; agencies	Regulated business; agencies
Estimated percentage of organizations practising today	15%	50%	20%	15%

Source: Grunig and Hunt (1984)

What is feedback?

Webster's definition of 'feedback' is 'the return to the point of origin, evaluative or corrective action, about an action or a process'. What this means in operational terminology is that it is possible to provide computer-tabulated information for managers about a firm's stakeholder practices and behaviour. Because this information is based on day-to-day perceptions it is a powerful tool for communication analysis, reflection and adjustment.

Feedback can be derived from two sources: those identified for a *generic* programme to help corporate communication managers focus on key behaviour of their audiences, and those identified on a *custom* basis where a number of activities or a particular group of stakeholders for the company are identified.

How does it work?

Feedback questionnaires and reports usually cover two areas, namely frequency and importance. *Frequency* is the extent to which the corporate communication manager uses a particular activity as perceived by the group or behaviours being evaluated.

Importance is the extent to which the corporate communication manager feels a particular activity, message or behaviour is important.

A typical feedback report will cover a section-by-section summary giving specific scores for each activity and a listing of the 'top ten' activities in order of importance with scores for each.

What are its applications?

Feedback provides three principal areas of application. Firstly, it can be used in *organizational surveys* to determine the extent to which a company is following practices which reflect or help to change the organization's culture. Secondly, it can be used on a *one-to-one counselling* basis where the process provides bottom-up or lateral feedback to supplement the top-down view usually proposed in dealing with journalists and/or employees. Thirdly, it can be used as a basis for a highly focused *training* where managers are helped to improve their communication performance in practice areas where deficiencies are evidenced. A typical research plan would include the research brief, the work plan, the data collection and analysis and evaluation. Given that every stakeholder group and every sub-group will have cultural differences of language, religion, values and attitudes, aesthetics, education and social organization, feedback is essential.

Public relations is difficult to describe in a simple statement. It is practised in organizations ranging from small to medium-sized enterprises to transnational, multinational corporations with budgets bigger than many Third World governments. Baskin *et al* (1997) define public relations as:

> Public relations is a management function that helps achieve organizational objectives, define philosophy and facilitate organizational change. Public relations practitioners communicate with all relevant internal and external publics to develop positive relationships and to create consistency between organizational goals and societal expectations. Public relations practitioners develop, execute and evaluate organizational programmes that promote the exchange of influence and understanding among an organization's constituent parts and publics.

❊ PUBLIC RELATIONS THEORY

Theories used in public relations can be summarized as follows:

I. Theories of relationships
    1. *Systems theory* – evaluates relationships and structure as they relate to the whole.
    2. *Situational theory* – situations define relationships.
    3. *Approaches to conflict resolution* – include separating people from the problem; focusing on interests, not positions; inventing options for mutual gain; and insisting on objective criteria.
II. Theories of cognition and behaviour
    4. *Action assembly theory* – understanding behaviour by understanding how people think.
    5. *Social exchange theory* – predicting behaviour of groups and individuals based on perceived rewards and costs.

6. *Diffusion theory* – people adopt an important idea or innovation after going through five discrete steps: awareness, interest, evaluation, trial and adoption.
7. *Social learning theory* – people use information processing to explain and predict behaviour.
8. *Elaborated likelihood model* – suggests decision making is influenced through repetition, rewards, and credible spokespersons.

III. Theories of mass communication

9. *Uses and gratification* – people are active users of media and select media based on its gratification for them.
10. *Agenda setting theory* – suggests that media content that people read, see, and listen to sets the agenda for society's discussion and interaction.

Probably the most pertinent area for confusion for the practitioner in respect of these theories is in the day-to-day management of brand image. Corporate image is as important as product brand image. Here, marketing uses the same channels of communication as the traditional public relations channels and often the same media. Both product branding and corporate image branding are concerned to move audience from awareness to a clearly defined perception that is seen to offer competitive or social advantage. (See Chapter 3 for a fuller discussion on brand image.)

POWER CONTROL AND PUBLIC RELATIONS

Strategic public relations is a power control model operating at the macro level and based around typical symmetrical models such as the one shown in Figure 1.2.

Most in-house practitioners know from experience that as counsellors they rarely make final strategic decisions or choices. This is usually made by the dominant coalition and thus, although all these factors may influence the choice of a model of strategic public relations, power control theory from organizational behaviour shows that the people who have power in an organization choose the type of public relations programmes that they do for reasons best known to them. The traditional view of the in-house practitioner having a board appointment in order to better

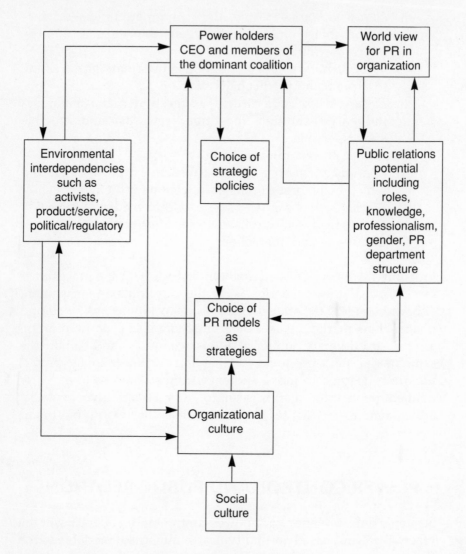

Figure 1.2 *Factors influencing choice of model*

Source: Grunig (1992)

influence board decision making is only sustainable if the practitioner is highly skilled and experienced in environmental management (ie management of the business environment), organizational behaviour and communication.

The box labelled 'World view for PR in organization' assumes that public relations is dominant in an organization but, as the arrows show, the world view for public relations is 'a product of the world view of the dominant coalition, the potential of the public relations department and the culture of the organization' (1992: 24). The arrow from environmental interdependencies to power holders indicates that 'managers gain power when they have knowledge and skills that help organizations manage crucial environmental interdependencies'. The arrow from power holders to environmental interdependencies indicates that 'the environment is in part at least the subjective perception of the dominant coalition'. The arrow from the choice of public relations models as strategies to the environment 'depicts the critical relationship between strategic management of public relations and organizational effectiveness'. The final two boxes 'depict the relationship among societal culture, organizational culture and excellence in public relations'.

PUBLIC RELATIONS AND ORGANIZATIONAL CULTURE

Organizational culture is created by the dominant coalition, especially by the founder or CEO of an organization, and managers do not gain influence if their values and ideology differ substantially from that of the organization. Organizational culture also is affected by the larger societal culture and by the environment. It affects public relations in the long term by moulding the world view for public relations and thus influences the choice of a model of public relations within an organization. While such a model identifies many of the variables essential to communication management and control, it also shows that if a culture is essentially hierarchical, authoritarian and reactive, the dominant coalition will generally choose an asymmetrical model of public relations. Furthermore, it will choose not to be counselled by the public relations expert who traditionally is not seen as having enough strategic awareness and is therefore of limited value. The strategic outcomes are shown in the evaluation diagram in Figure 1.3.

RESEARCH

Art vs science

Most management disciplines that are well regarded are founded in established practices which are well researched. The lack of a research base has been a hindrance to public relations. Specifically, how to measure the effects of the public relations contribution has been a long-standing concern.

A more scientific approach to evaluation is emerging based on developments from media studies and more specifically from both audience research tools and techniques, and development in technology. They provide essential information for the justification of the public relations budget through evaluation of strategic public relations programmes. The Dozier model shown in Figure 1.3 provided a conceptual matrix by which practitioners could classify and report the impact of their activities based on subjective or objective criteria.

		Content of evaluation		
		Preparation	Dissemination	Impact
Individualistic		Communication activities prepared via application of internalized professional standards of quality	Dissemination of messages evaluated by reactions of mass media professionals	Impact of PR activities evaluated via subjective qualitative 'sense' of publics' reactions
Scientific		Communication activities prepared via application of scientifically derived knowledge of publics	Dissemination of messages evaluated by quantified measures of media usage of messages	Impact of PR activities evaluated via objective, quantitative measure of publics' reactions

Figure 1.3 *Content and method in evaluation*

Source: Dozier, in Grunig (1992)

Evaluation and research also play an increasingly important role in the underpinning of strategic public relations systems and processes through the systematic gathering, recording and analysing of data relating to image, identity, reputation and perception by all stakeholders having an interest in the success or development of an organization. These include research into such elements as advertising effectiveness, media efficacy and corporate image, both internally and externally.

As the sources of information grow and become more easily accessible (government statistics, business directories, specialist digests and pocket books, international data, specialized trade periodicals, Internet databases etc), decision making improves all the time. Added to this is the improved quality of industrial and other surveys, including attitude surveys, field surveys and interviews. Because an organization has a wide range of individuals and groups who exist as stakeholders, this is the area that is most often outsourced by the internal public relations strategist.

However, as a professional player, you may not be aware that you will have a major role to play in the strategy process and your evaluation skills may need to extend well beyond those set by the requirements of the public relations function. You will be aware that, in successful companies, structures are constantly changing and that executives' knowledge and daily contact with operations, the marketplace and consultancies create an ever-evolving strategy formulation process. At public relations conferences and meetings, workshops and committees, people talk to each other from competing companies, suppliers and customers and in this way often learn about the first signs of significant developments from the bottom up. A typical enquiry at such times from consultants and trainers is why it is necessary to address strategy formation and strategy implication which are longer-term activities when the role of the public relations consultant is to deal with the here and now.

The implementation of a communication strategy is often not thought out until the business strategy has been adopted by a main board or other senior management. Implementation is then sometimes left to the operating people without clear guidelines. The top-down approach often ignores the contribution that public relations can make, given their knowledge about change in the external environment and the knowledge gained by interaction with stakeholders in that environment.

At a strategic level, public relations affects the whole organization and so inevitably, the involvement of all top management is crucial for success. At an operational or tactical level, the need for specialist practitioners knowledgeable of public relations techniques is crucial and needs to be coordinated and managed competently, particularly at the point of decision making. Tactical decisions have to be seen to fit into corporate or business objectives.

SUMMARY

This chapter defines the concept of public relations, identifies its strategic nature by integrating it within the corporate strategy-making process, and defines its role and practice within organizations.

CASE STUDY: CENTRAIS DE APOIO AOS TRANSPORTES (CAT), BRAZIL

Published by kind permission of IPRA.

Introduction

In 1997, this company was required to design, build and manage a hazardous local terminal in the district of Paulínia, São Paulo, Brazil. This would allow trucks to access Replan, an oil refinery, by reducing irregular and dangerous parking on surrounding roads. A public relations campaign was undertaken for CAT to encourage drivers to use the new terminal.

This case illustrates the points raised in the preceding chapter as follows:

● The campaign strategy included consultation with numerous stakeholder groups simultaneously.
● The cost factor brought added value to the campaign strategy.
● The impact of media relations went beyond resolution of the initial problem.
● The benefits of creating a public relations campaign as opposed, say, to an advertising campaign are articulated.

CENTRAIS DE APOIO AOS TRANSPORTES

The problem

Paulínia is a small district in the countryside of the State of São Paulo, 114 km from the capital. Replan, a refinery responsible for processing 20 per cent of Brazil's oil by-products, is based in that city. Close by, the distributors – such as Shell, Esso, Texaco, Ipiranga and BR – have support bases for the truck drivers who come to pick up fuels.

Trucks entered the Replan site irregularly and in a disorderly manner. Every day, about 1,800 vehicles with hazardous loads were parked on the margin of the highway that crosses the city (SP-332 highway): 20–40-ton trucks with three and six axles. In order to load, they parked anywhere they could – both on the SP-332 highway and on the streets of the city of Paulínia. The average waiting time, for loading and leaving, was six hours.

The irregular parking posed extreme risk to the local community and to the environment. It caused accidents on the highway, blocked the traffic, polluted the ground and, in particular, contaminated the municipality's water-table. Furthermore, there was no basic infrastructure for waiting truckers. Truck drivers were exposed to robberies and hold-ups; had no basic facilities for health, leisure and personal hygiene; and were unable to contact their families.

In 1994, municipal law 1822/94 was enacted. It stipulated that vehicles carrying oil by-products, whether loaded or not, could only park at a Hazardous Load Terminal which was to be built in the yards of the load distributors or in the parking areas of the carriers. Truckers had to comply with the safety regulations laid down by the law.

The contract for building the Hazardous Load Terminal was put out to public tender and the winning consortium, CAT – Centrais de Apoio aos Transportes – was then responsible for designing, building and managing it. It was commissioned in July 1997, with capacity for 558 trucks, and complied with the strictest safety norms.

A Centre for Support to Truck Drivers was also built, offering the truck drivers rest, leisure, personal hygiene, food and communal facilities during waiting periods. This compound cost about US$12 million, and generated 120 direct jobs.

Within six months of opening, however, the truck drivers still did not use the terminal, and the municipal authorities did not force them to comply with the law. During the month of February 1998, only 66 trucks parked there. In March 1998 a public relations agency – Assessoria de Comunicações (ADS) – was hired. Their objective was to save the undertaking – 90 employees had already been fired.

Research

By collecting assessments from experts and comparing the case of Paulínia with experiences in other cities and countries, the ADS team identified several key problem areas:

- The undertaking had been implemented with no prior awareness and motivation work with the truck drivers.
- Contacts with the distributors had involved no effort to establish partnerships, but rather intimidated them with hints of possible fines.
- The name chosen – Paulicentro – gave the impression of a parking area for trucks and not of a terminal for hazardous loads. This made the drivers think that this was provided courtesy of the City Administration with no obligation on them.
- The introductory 'no charge' incentive in the first month reinforced the expectation among truck drivers that they would receive services free of charge.

A survey of the truck drivers was carried out, and showed that they were rejecting the Paulicentro for the following reasons:

- It was expensive – an average stay of six hours cost US $18, while leaving the truck on the highway cost nothing.
- The managers were arrogant.
- Meals cost twice as much as those sold by independent road-side operators.
- They considered it a common parking area, which should be free.
- They felt isolated in a huge terminal where they found few fellow drivers.

Planning

From this analysis, the consultancy decided to focus on several areas:

- It was necessary for the municipal and state authorities to take their own responsibilities seriously.
- It should be explained to the drivers that the terminal was not an additional and pointless expense, but rather an improvement in their own quality of life and a necessity for the community of Paulínia.
- The community press were natural allies that should be called upon to actively support the campaign.
- Finally, dialogue was necessary between the carriers and distributors.

The ideal, to maximize the impact, was that the programme should build up on several fronts simultaneously, thus generating a snowball effect which would overcome resistance.

Implementation

In April 1998, the agency went on the offensive. The name of Paulicentro was changed to Hazardous Load Terminal. Employees were made aware of the importance of giving a warm and friendly service to clients to create a pleasant and welcoming environment. The restaurant started to charge a promotional price, the same US $3 which the truck drivers spent with the food stands on the sides of the highway.

The soccer World Cup, in June 1998, offered a good opportunity to show off the new look of the truck drivers' terminal. Leaflets were distributed which invited truck drivers to see the Brazil games in the comfort of the truck drivers' support centre, with free parking at the terminal on these days. However, it was realized that even if the number of trucks increased, it would not make drivers feel at home because they were accustomed to enjoying the action highlights with many relatives and friends. The consultants chose a regional journalist – the former editor of the main local newspaper – to act as social adviser. His credibility convinced the press that the terminal had the only facilities capable of properly handling vehicles with hazardous loads in Paulínia. He obtained sympathetic support from the newspapers for the undertaking. Thus, the statements which the agency had been making, suggesting that Paulínia's water-table could be polluted, received emphasis in the news. The suspicion that they were drinking contaminated water worried a great number of Paulínia's inhabitants.

Awareness work was also undertaken with the hauliers' trade union, emphasizing the social responsibility of the drivers and the necessity that they should not harm the communities with which they interact.

In April 1998 strict fines established by the new Brazilian Traffic Code were applied, signs were placed in Paulínia to warn truck drivers that the new fine for irregular parking in the public highways was equal to 30 days' stay at the terminal, and that three of these fines would lead to the suspension of their driving licence for several months. The agency considered it fundamental to make a deal with one large distributor which would serve as an example for the others. Thus, for eight months ADS negotiated with the vice-president of Shell and the general directors of Shell's two carrier companies. It offered, on behalf of CAT, subsidized prices for Shell truck drivers for one year. Once this proposal had been accepted, the remaining distributors, one by one, started to accept the same terms. And, with the 450 trucks linked to

Shell, there were enough drivers to create a communal environment at the terminal.

A comic-strip primer was produced by the agency, which explained the issues involved. This was distributed to the community. The consultants also sought the help of opinion-formers in the community, such as the priest, the prosecutor, association leaders, etc. These citizens gave their support to the cause.

Accidents on the SP-332 were given substantial publicity to show the community the real dimension of the problem. Facts that hitherto had remained almost unnoticed started to be highlighted by the press and noted by the community who became justifiably indignant.

To make irregular parking more difficult, CAT, guided by the agency, bore the costs of placing pickets at the median strip and on the hard shoulder of the highway. Finally, contact with the authorities became regular and resistant. From the Paulínia Security Department, for instance, a commitment was obtained to enforce the traffic laws of the municipality. Thus, truck drivers who parked irregularly close to the highways started to be fined. Many of them, however, evaded the fines by parking on the highway itself, the supervision of which is a State responsibility. The Public Security Secretary of Paulínia then, in regional TV interviews arranged by ADS, publicly declared that his Department was performing its duties but that the State was not. The news annoyed the State Highway Police who claimed that they had no funds to install a police station in Paulínia or to acquire the required police cars. Once again, CAT bore these costs with the agreement of the Public Security Department of the State.

After months of negotiations with the State authorities, the effects of yet more traffic accidents at the SP-332 highway made the Public Security Secretary of São Paulo decide to act decisively. He called all the parties involved to a meeting in Paulínia and gave them a deadline – 2 February 1999 – for the traffic and environmental laws to be strictly complied with.

Evaluation

The results of the campaign can be measured by the number of trucks parked at the terminal every month. There were 155 in March 1998, but the number more than doubled in the following month (358),and went into four figures in September 1998 (1,525). It remained at this level until the Public Security Department of the State checked it and, in February 1999, it leapt to 5,445. In March 1999, a figure of 7,349 trucks was reached. An increase of 4,640 per cent in 13 months!

The hazardous load terminal, which was almost closed, is now fully recovered and has consolidated its position. There is a consensus among the authorities and the community of Paulínia that, without the campaign, the terminal would have closed and the region would have lost precious jobs during a difficult time for the Brazilian economy.

It was an opportunity to associate the interests of a company with the benefits of the wider community. The campaign brought more safety and improved the quality of life for the inhabitants of Paulínia; it saved lives and gave the truck drivers improved conditions.

2

A place on the board: public relations strategy in a professional context

Public relations practice is generally driven by analysis and research of stakeholders. Stakeholder audiences demand meaningful messages from internal and external communication. Organizations deal with pressures and developments from both internal and external drivers, usually concurrently, but it is often only in times of crisis that an organization values public relations input. Most corporate decision making distinguishes between objective and subjective interpretation of events, takes a continuous view of change rather than reacting immediately to turbulent or sudden change and approaches corporate strategy as a process involving choices rather than determinate positions. Managing public relations strategic decision making is no different and, like accounting or law, has its own body of knowledge, rules and regulations.

Public relations has traditionally relied on case studies and empirical research to provide a base on which to draw and develop models of theory and best practice. Few practitioner writers adopt a polemical position about the communication aspects of public relations, yet, like most fledgling disciplines or professions, they are criticized for being too descriptive and banal. An upsurge in the number of public relations research consultancies and an increase in client billings are an indication of recognition of the need for proven expertise. Clients increasingly want to extract value for money and insist on measured justification for public relations expenditure.

PROACTIVE PROCESSES

If practitioners are to analyse the pressures and problems confronting the employing organization or company, then it is understood that a number of proactive processes must take place. These include:

- using a variety of methods of collating data including CD ROM library indexes and other organizational sources and external reference materials;
- different interpretations of the problem which incorporate perceptions of target audiences, including the media;
- the extent to which it is possible to define and predict future trends and change;
- the contribution of managers and employees as a resource in meeting the public relations campaign or corporate communication objectives.

Commonly referred to as environmental scanning, the public relations specialist will investigate and analyse internal and external pressures, diagnose problems confronting the organization, suggest future trends and developments and propose or counsel prescriptions for future action and, in the case of crisis management, remedial action.

The SIDEC model shown in Figure 2.1 gives the strategic public

The sidec model gives the Strategic public

relations manager a focus for choosing a particular type of communication policy, by analysing the firm's corporate strategy in relation to the similarity or otherwise of the driving forces affecting the firm's mission, the amount or nature of control exercised by the board directors and the scale of environmental pressure on the organization.

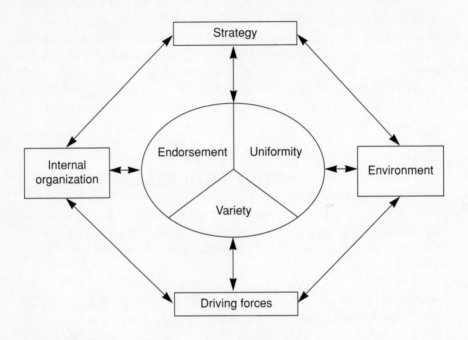

Figure 2.1 *Factors in the choice of policy*

Source: Van Riel (1995)

One of the criticisms of the corporate strategy literature is that it makes little distinction in some cases between different organizations in terms of their ownership, organization and objectives. Clearly, private companies, voluntary bodies and public services adopt different approaches to their organization and objectives, but this is reflected more in the culture of each organization rather than the process of communication. The fundamental nature of human communication may be universal, but for the PRO, message style and delivery may change to best fit the culture in which it is being set.

STRATEGIC MANAGEMENT MODELS AND PUBLIC RELATIONS

Perhaps the most famous of all strategic management models is the Johnson and Scholes model first published in 1984, adapted in 1997 (Johnson and Scholes, 1984) as shown in Figure 2.2, and applied below to operational activities.

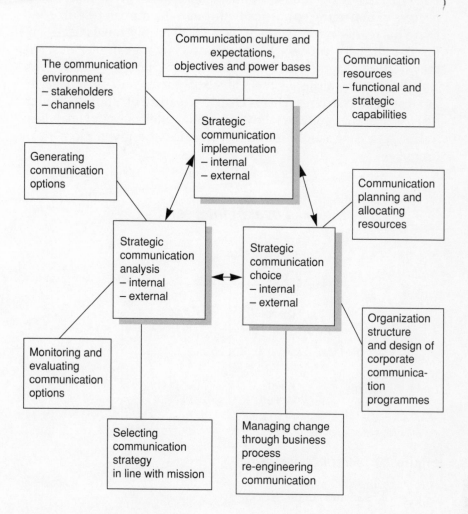

Figure 2.2 *Applying corporate strategy to corporate communication*

Source: Oliver (1997). Adapted from Johnson and Scholes (1984)

It is important to recognize that there are a number of weaknesses in this model, or at least potentials for misunderstanding. While the model shows the essential elements of the strategy process, it is not linear, starting at the establishment of a mission and ending with implementation. As all competent public relations practitioners know, these processes must run in parallel and with consideration of resources and the practicalities of implementation. In later texts Johnson and Scholes attempt to discuss the process of managing strategically through the human resource and make the reader more aware of the tactical requirements necessary for the strategy process to be effective. For example, in 1993, they included a model of stakeholder mapping to characterize stakeholders in terms of their level of power and their level of interest in an outcome. This is clearly a feature of 'spin-doctoring' discussed earlier and the following model offers a useful analytical tool in assessing communication priorities at a given moment in time.

Level of interest

		Low	High
Power	Low	Minimal effort	Keep informed
	High	Keep satisfied	Keep players

Figure 2.3 *Stakeholder mapping*

Source: Johnson and Scholes (1993)

This approach suggests that, although mission statements articulate organizational objectives and these objectives derive from economic managerial or social responsibility considerations, stakeholders have expectations which may not always be met. These expectations relate to the performance of the organization as well as being influenced by the external cultural context in which the organization is operating. Stakeholders have different degrees of power to determine the objectives of an organization and various levels of interest in exercising that power, and so stakeholder objectives affect the development of future organizational strategies.

The process of business re-engineering in the 1980s concentrated on an update of the challenge to think about what we do and how we do it. The systems approach to management is not just a process of analysis and reductionism but a process of linking things together, the process of synthesis. In the 1990s, Johnson and Scholes produced a model for analysing organizational culture which they argued was essential if synthesis was to occur. They referred to the interplay of various factors in organizational culture as the cultural web or the mind-set of an organization – that is to say, the way it sees itself and its environment, as shown in Figure 2.4 which links together formal and informal ways that organizational systems work through important relationships (structure); core groupings (power); measurement and rewind systems (control); behavioural norms (stories); training (rituals); language and livery (symbols); process and expected competencies (routine).

It is these factors that make up a paradigm; for example, the organizational paradigm lies at the heart of any public relations change strategy because it describes a set of preconceptions which underlie people's way of looking at the world in general, not just the organization. It comprises a set of assumptions which people rarely question. From time to time the paradigm is shaken up and a paradigm shift takes place.

In such an event, textbooks have to be rewritten as a paradigm shift involves the rethinking of basic assumptions underlying people's perceptions. Paradigm shifts, that is, fundamental changes in the ruling paradigm, are rarely dramatic in business and management, although electronic communications and global technology generally may be said to have changed the

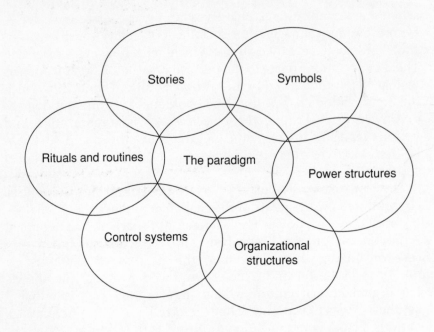

Figure 2.4 *Assessing corporate culture*

Source: Johnson and Scholes (1993)

ruling paradigm of strategic public relations theory and practice, hence the subtitle of this book.

Systems and processes, particularly in respect of media relations, are working under an underlying set of assumptions and beliefs which have changed and are undergoing a revolutionary paradigm shift. There are few organizations where managers are allowed to differ openly from or criticize the official line on strategy and policy and yet this may lie at the heart of the public relations expert counsel. Adherence to the accepted way of running the organization and the markets within which the organization is operating may not be openly criticized, while internal communications attempt to reinforce the official line through the company newsletter, for example.

ORDINARY AND EXTRAORDINARY PUBLIC RELATIONS MANAGEMENT

The Stacey (1991) approach to strategy takes the conflicts inherent in any organizational debate about cultural differences and provides a model of ordinary and extraordinary management. Modern models of strategy formulation stress the instability of the relationship between an organization and its environment because time and dynamic never stand still. In any organization there is a perceived need to maintain stability and harmony while making sure that the organization can change in order to survive. This contradiction is expressed by Stacey as ordinary management on the one hand and extraordinary management on the other. These are useful concepts to critically appraise the role of public relations in corporate strategy. They reflect the fundamental philosophy of public relations in that the overall corporate message must be consistent (ordinary management) while monitoring changes in stakeholder perceptions that could impact on corporate objectives (extraordinary management) and which in turn lead to changes in the message.

The challenge for strategic public relations is to accept widely that, for efficient operation at any given time, it is necessary for an organization to have a clear sense of purpose and unity, but also a parallel culture in which it is possible to raise safely a variety of viewpoints to challenge complacency and ensure survival. Clinical psychology tells us that it is important that cognitive feedback loops operate in a positive manner so that perception and communication can be updated and clarified where appropriate. This is the basis of the symmetrical models promoted by Grunig *et al*.

Public relations choices are on the basis of rational criteria, but this is only possible when there is agreement on what the business is all about and what kind of environment it is having to cope with. Stacey argues that managers only operate within bounded rationality. The complexities of modern organizations mean that they have to adopt a pragmatic approach to decision making and accept that they cannot conceptualize or accommodate all possibilities. Bureaucratic procedures help to simplify the manager's task, providing rules and procedures for tackling many decisions. A hierarchical management structure ensures that difficult decisions can be made within the context of the prevailing ideology – the official line of the ruling coalition.

Ordinary management

This description of ordinary management is necessary to ensure that targets can be met and that the organization survives through rational processes. It presupposes a stable environment and can only be practised in contained change situations. It is not a negative concept given that it must be practised if an organization is to be able to control and deliver competitive advantage. It also implies that public relations, however, is conducted on the basis of asymmetrical communication in which the organization 'gets what it wants without changing its behaviour or without compromising' (Grunig and White, 1992). The asymmetric nature of public relations means that the organization will find it difficult to adapt to a changing environment because it does not recognize that communication with the outside, as well as its own employees, must be a two-way process. Stacey's (1993) definition of extraordinary management states that it is 'the use of intuitive, political, group learning modes of decision-making and self-organizing forms of control in open-ended change situations. It is the form of management that managers must use if they are to change strategic direction and innovate' (1993: 72).

Extraordinary management

Despite the potential dangers for organizations remaining exclusively dedicated to ordinary management, a closer look at what is involved in extraordinary management will explain British reticence. Extraordinary management involves questioning and shattering paradigms and then creating new ones. It is a process which depends critically on contradiction and tension. The changing of paradigms is a revolutionary rather than an evolutionary process and cannot be intended by the organization. Stacey argues that both forms of management have to coexist if the organization is to evolve and survive a changing environment. An organization needs to provide a stable basis for meeting its short-term objectives and targets while at the same time providing a basis for transforming itself in the future to respond to changes in the environment. Some organizations fail to recognize the need to allow for extraordinary management and instead rely on radical changes of chief executives, consultants and other outside change agents who have little understanding of the problems of the organization. This is where the public relations consultant has to be particularly aware and cautious of the conflicting demands that may be put upon service provision. Many practitioners argue that they do what they're asked, no more no less, within the brief and the fee. In that they are professionally pragmatic, but that approach is not conducive to being consciously aware of where a particular service provision fits into the overall scheme of things for monitoring and evaluating the wider environment.

The implications of ordinary management for public relations are familiar through relationships with major stakeholders. For example:

- Shareholders – the annual report. For most shareholders asymmetrical communication of results will tend to apply, whereas with major institutional shareholders self-interest will dictate a degree of symmetrical communication and a genuine desire to listen to their concerns will be essential and generally implemented.
- Customers – the marketing and sales departments will tend to dominate in this aspect of the public relations role but, increasingly, symmetrical communication is being recognized as being essential to obtain competitive advantage through so-called relationship marketing. A long-term two-way relationship may be established with customers to allow for feedback into marketing strategy. Grant and Schlesinger (1995) developed the concept of 'value exchange' in which a company optimizes the relationship between the financial investment a company makes in particular customer relationships and the return that customers generate by the specific way they choose to respond to the company's offering. For this, a careful attention to the behaviour of customers is essential.
- Employees – the ruling coalition within the organization can of course use a wide range of channels to communicate with employees in order to achieve the aim or harmony, fit or convergence to a particular configuration and to ensure that

they share the same mental models or paradigms. Posters that repeat the published mission statement, memos, messages contained in the actions of management relating to discipline suggestions and so on all contribute to an overall strategic process.

Implications of ordinary and extraordinary management

The implications of extraordinary management for public relations are significant. The need for extraordinary management in order for the organization to survive and flourish in an unstable environment has been emphasized, but control of the extraordinary process has to be achieved by informal organization of its activities. As the formal organization exists to protect the paradigm, the status quo, managers who wish to change the paradigm have to operate within an informal organization in informal groups which they organize themselves. These groups can cope with uncertainty and ambiguity, anathema to the formal bureaucracy, and tap each other's perceptions of what is going on in the organization. According to Stacey, these groups are essentially political in nature. People handle conflicting interests through persuasion and negotiation, implicit bargaining of one person's contribution or interests for another's, and power exerted by means of influence rather than authority. This informal system has been referred to as the network system and often lies at the heart of public relations expertise. These can coexist with hierarchy and bureaucracy, but must be encouraged by the actions of the bureaucracy and supported by top management.

When organizations manage to combine ordinary with extraordinary management successfully to create an innovative culture while maintaining stability, a sound public relations strategy plays a core role in sustaining the firm's corporate strategy. Both support competitive advantage while ensuring the capability to ward off hostile competition, pressure groups and media.

The concept of extraordinary management may lead to groups within the organization attempting to undermine the control of the organization and, ultimately, the ability of the organization to adapt requires that subversive activity takes place without control being lost. Decisions are not made by organizations as such, but rather by dominant coalitions within organizations, and these coalitions are not likely to be defined clearly in the official organization chart. White and Dozier (1992) argue that dominant coalitions still need information to help them make decisions. This is frequently provided by boundary spanners, individuals within the organization who frequently interact with the organization's environment... and relay information to the dominant coalition.

VISUAL IDENTITY

The cultural web plays an important part in understanding corporate identity and a visual identity step model might look something like Table 2.1.

Table 2.1   *A visual identity step model*

Corporate Identity	Objectives	Key issue	Methodology
Situation analysis	Analysing corporate expression and customer impressions	Determining perception of the firms and competitors' aesthetic output	Corporate expressions/customer impressions research
Designing the aesthetics-strategy	Creating distinct impactive aesthetic impressions	Selecting strategically appropriate styles and themes	The styles and themes inventory
Building the collection of design elements	Implementing the strategy with rules of balance	Organising and managing the implementation	The aesthetics balance sheet
Aesthetics quality control	Monitoring, tracking and adjusting corporate aesthetics over time	Evaluation of prior outputs in the framework and fine-tuning including updating	Aesthetics impact tracking

Nicholas Ind says:

> A corporate brand is more than just the outward manifestation of
> an organization, its name, logo, visual presentation. Rather it is
> the core of values that defines it... Communications must be
> based on substance. If they are not, inconsistency creeps in and
> confusion follows shortly thereafter... What defines the corporation
> in comparison with the brand is the degree of complexity. It
> is larger, more diverse and has several audiences that it must
> interact with. The corporate brand must be able to meet the
> needs of the often competing claims of its stakeholders. To
> achieve that it must have clarity of vision, of values and of leader-
> ship. (1997: 13)

The strategic challenge for most organizations today is adapting
their structures and culture to achieve sound relationships built
on long-term mutual advantage through the integration of
internal and external communication. The principles and techniques of public relations contribute to all strategic areas of an
organization. Stakeholder groups are segmented into target audiences for monitoring, measuring and controlling specific messages
which must meet functional objectives while attaining corporate
consistency.

The critical role of communication in operationalizing corporate
mission and translating it into reality, and the importance of vision
in the achievement of corporate objectives, are based on perception
as a measurable variable of reality. Strategic planning models
relate to public relations planning through open systems theory
and general management tools such as hard-line (not necessarily
bottom line) value-added concepts. Many public relations professionals will argue that this is not new; such factors have always
existed as benchmarks for justifying their intangible but critical
contribution. The difference today is that IT capability produces a
variety of identifiable factors which can be seen to be part of an
organization's intellectual capital, if not essential to its survival on
occasions. The public relations expert acts as specialist counsel to a
corporate boardroom and its specialist input is fundamental to
management in sourcing, analysing, assessing, managing and
tracking information and translating that information for the
benefit of the corporate whole. Through flexibility and change,
organizations have to be flexible, changing, lifelong learning organizations which encourage effective symmetrical communication

to such an extent that external audiences such as media and dominant political coalitions can influence or even drive strategy from time to time.

BENCHMARKING

Public relations strategy, like any other variable corporate planning, must be able to identify measurable performance indicators. An eight-factor model is suggested as shown in Figure 2.5, which

Figure 2.5   *Performance indicators*

Source: Oliver (1977)

at the time of going to press, was still being worked on in respect of quantifying evidence for a national standard of organizational public relations performance.

BOUNDARY SPANNERS

Public relations professionals as boundary spanners play an important role in translating meaning from and about the organization in relation to the environment. They must often counsel top management about its implicit assumptions. White and Dozier (1992) quote the case of a logging company which might view trees as a crop to be harvested rather than a natural resource to be cherished. Indeed, the logging company's traditional world view is embedded in their language as, for example, when they refer to 'timber stands', a term implying that trees are there to be harvested like 'strands' of corn. During a symmetrical communication process, conflict between the organization and environmental pressure groups can be forestalled if PROs fulfil their role as boundary spanners by ensuring that there is a two-way exchange of information between the organization, the groups involved and the wider, often media-led environment.

In another example from local government, the dominant and ruling left-wing coalition within a local authority might have a world view which saw the borough for which they are responsible as consisting of needy people in need of subsidy and support. A different, say right-wing, group might view the situation as one consisting of council taxpayers (local taxes) being burdened with council tax payments and resenting money going to needy people exempt from paying council tax. In this latter case, the public relations task would be to increase awareness and modify the uni-dimensional view of the dominant coalition while simultaneously communicating the needs of the poor to the ratepayers within the community.

FORWARD PLANNING

The public relations search for strategic factors in the environment cannot ignore the future, however difficult it is to assess. There are innumerable cases of organizations which failed to spot the changes looming up in the future which threatened them or which provided opportunities for development which were taken up early by competitors. McMaster (1996) says that the past is a poor basis for predicting the future, an aim which is in any case not attainable. What organizations can do is to see the structure of the future by examining the structure and process of the present. McMaster is stressing that, although it is impossible to predict the detail of the future, the structure of the future is a set of relationships within a complex system which is constantly adapting; for example, the relationships with technology and other forces which are affecting the environment within which the organization operates. The challenge of foresight is the 'vast space of possibility' and McMaster cites 3M's success in organizing for foresight. New products form a very high percentage of its product range at any one time. These products have arisen not only from individual acts of foresight but rather from an organizational design and management culture which continually encourages new products. In other words, the organization is itself the source of invention.

The starting point for the development of strategy has usually involved a systematic analysis of the organization's environment, often from an analysis of external factors. Popular models are based on PESTLE, the interaction between factors in politics, economics, society, technology, law and ecology. Such models are beginning to appear static, with a tendency to drive out more positive visions of what the future might hold for a particular organization.

TANGIBLE AND INTANGIBLE CAPITAL

Inevitably, however, any vision of the future will depend on resources and the strategic importance of a focus on resources arises because it can be argued that, ultimately, profits can be seen as a return to the resources controlled and owned by the firm. However, resources can be divided into tangible and intangible resources. For each of these, there are usually key indicators, or a way of measuring their value. Public relations practitioners have often been caught in a mire of confusion in an attempt to offer hard measurement of intangible outcomes. Intangible resources, which

39

do not appear on the balance sheet, are difficult to value objectively, even when recognized as being of value. Sometimes their value can be inferred when an acquisition takes place, the difference between the book valuation and the purchase price being denoted confusingly as goodwill arising on acquisition. Putting a value to a recognized brand name which is held in good esteem is a case in point.

The IPR definition of public relations as the planned and sustained effort to establish and 'maintain goodwill' and mutual understanding between an organization and its publics is no longer enough. Goodwill has to be measured and accounted for and thus we see the recent rise in research and evaluation of corporate identity image and reputation. Brooking's (1996) classification of resources breaks down intellectual capital into market assets, human-centred assets, infrastructure assets and intellectual property assets. On the other hand, Quinn *et al* (1996) sees the professional intellect as operating on four levels of cognitive knowledge, advanced know-how, systems understanding and self-motivated creativity, which he regards as the highest level of intellect reflecting motivation and adaptability. Petrash (1996) describes the approach to intellectual capital management adopted by the Dow Chemical Company as defining intellectual capital as a formula:

Intellectual capital = Human capital + Organizational capital + Customer capital

We might say public relations strategy = corporate or external communication + internal or HR communication + marketing or customer communication. At the Dow Chemical Company they have over 75 multi-functional intellectual asset management teams which meet to review the patent portfolio. These are led by intellectual asset managers who in turn report to the intellectual management function. The whole is supported by an intellectual management centre which provides, for example, database support, career development of managers and sharing of best practice. What we are seeing then is a resource-driven approach to strategy based on the view that sustainable competitive advantage is derived from an identification of the firm's existing and future strategic capability. The long-term dynamic nature of a public relations strategy is that it is

responsive to changes in the environment and often requires identification of existing and future communication gaps which need
to be filled.

PRESENTING ALLIANCES

One area of strategic public relations expertise of increasing
importance is in managing the public relations activity
surrounding the outcomes of strategic alliances which have
become an important financial option for organizations. These
involve relationships between organizations which fall short of
merger but which may go as far as mutual equity stakes, each
organization owning a minority of shares in the other. On the
other hand, they may involve no more than limited cooperation
and consultation between otherwise bitter rivals but either
way, the financial press will take a close interest. These alliances
do not just involve very large organizations. No organization
whatever its size can any longer hope to acquire all the skills
and competencies necessary for operating in a global environment
and it must therefore attempt to fill the gaps by working with
other companies in partnership. The types of alliances that
can arise are licences, joint ventures, franchising, private label
agreements, buyer/seller arrangements or the forging of
common standards and consortia. A prerequisite for a successful
alliance is that there must be a clear purpose and objective for
the arrangement and the process must be managed according to
schedule and without loss of control. The role of the public
relations strategist will be to ensure that media coverage does not
give the organizations involved loss of control of their own
destinies.

It would be interesting to see how long the strategic alliance
approach lasts. For example, there are already claims that Japanese
companies rarely commit their best scientists and engineers to
MITI-sponsored projects, while IBM set up a special facility in
Japan where Fujitsu could test its new mainframe software before
considering a licensing agreement. This provided some protection
against loss of technological know-how through an alliance.
Brouthers *et al* (1995) have a set of guidelines to be considered,
namely complementary skills, cooperative cultures, compatible
goals and commensurate levels of risk – what they call the Four Cs

of successful international strategic alliances. Gugler (1992) shows the complex of alliances formed by Philips, which brings new meaning to the concept of corporate image, identity and reputation (Figure 2.6).

Strategy in its classical sense is a competitive model which aims to enhance the value of an organization to its shareholders. An organization chooses between strategic options which may include mergers and divestments. Public relations strategists may be involved in merger acquisitions to increase shareholder value: merger acquisitions' decision-making process, post-merger implementations and corporate divestment programmes.

The trend for a reversal of the movement towards growth has led to the break-up of corporations with the intention of releasing shareholder value and so, in a turbulent environment, organizations have to include in their range of strategic options a consideration of research and development. This is often seen as a cost rather than an investment in the United Kingdom and, as with public relations programmes, there are disagreements about the extent to which expenditure should be subjected to vigorous cost–benefit analysis. Given that the emphasis is on producing down-sized companies which outsource many of the essential functions such as public relations, the issue of innovation and the virtual company cannot be ignored (Chesborough and Teece, 1996).

ETHICS

One central area of importance to the theory and practice of strategic public relations is ethics, which is encapsulated in the IPR's professional code of conduct, and worth considering in the light of stakeholder theory as shown in Table 2.2.

Increasingly, communications experts and public relations practitioners find themselves involved in mediation, conflict resolution and relationship or personal communication development programmes. Clifford Christians and Michael Traeber (1997) identified a broad-based ethical theory of communication which transcends cultures and the world of mass media. They believed it could be accepted by society as a whole and that organizations would find it possible to adopt it and adapt it to form the basis of organizational codes. Christians and Traeber demonstrate that 'certain ethical protonorms – above all truth telling, commitment

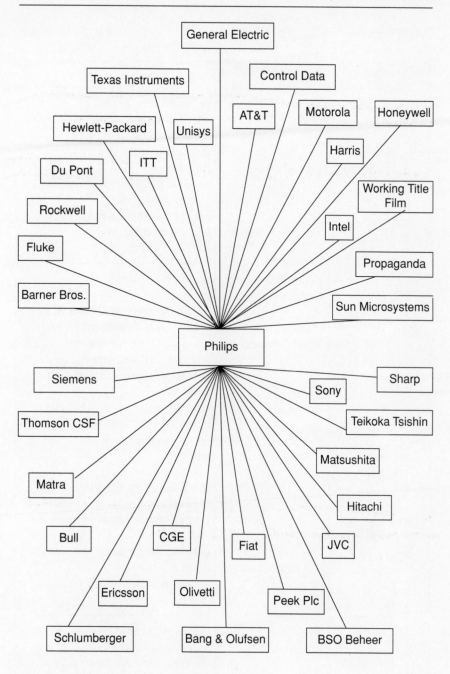

Figure 2.6 *Philips alliance network*

Source: Engler (1992)

Table 2.2 *Stakeholders' responsibilities*

Stakeholders	Responsibilities	
1. Customers	Economic issues:	profitability competitive products survival of the company product quality
	Ethical issues:	honesty the best possible products and services satisfy customer needs
	Voluntary issues:	long-term business function development
2. Employees	Economic issues:	work and income
	Legal issues:	cooperation following the regulations in dismissal situations
	Ethical issues:	good working conditions stability and security developing possibilities honesty
	Voluntary issues:	education supporting activities and interests

3. Competitors	Ethical issues:	truthful
		    information
		fair marketing and pricing
		    practices
		no use of questionable practices
		consistency and stability
		playing the game by the rules

	Voluntary issues:	good relations cooperation in industry-related issues
4. Owners	Economic issues:	return on assets/investments securing investments maximizing cash flow solvency profits
	Ethical issues:	adequate information

5.	Suppliers	Economic issues:	volumes
			profitability
		Ethical issues:	honesty
		Voluntary issues:	sustainable and reliable long term relations
6.	Community	Economic issues:	taxes
			employment
		Legal issues:	influence on trade balance
		Ethical issues:	following laws and regulations
		Voluntary issues:	behaving with integrity
			supporting local activities
7.	Government	Economic issues:	taxes
			employment
			influence on trade balance
		Legal issues:	following laws and
		Ethical issues:	regulations
			behaving with integrity
		Voluntary issues:	supporting local activities
8.	Financial groups	Economic issues:	profitability
			security of investment
		Ethical issues:	adequate information
9.	The environment eg pressure groups	Legal issues:	compliance with environmental regulations
		Ethical issues:	environmental friendliness
			protecting the environment
			product recycling
		Voluntary issues:	proactive environmental management
10.	Media and press	Legal issues:	compliance with the law, eg invasion of privacy
		General issues:	compliance with Guidelines, Codes of Conduct and Ethics Statements
		Voluntary issues:	Internal Web pages and chat rooms

Source: Adapted from Aurila (1993), cited in Oliver (1997)

to justice, freedom in solidarity and respect for human dignity – are validated as core values in communications in different cultures'. They conclude that 'we are in search of the ultimate and unconditional characteristics of human life, from which the meaning of human actions can be derived. Communication is one such act.'

The development and pre-testing of the means for achieving ethical objectives through research is one factor in the developing assessment framework discussed earlier. Pre-tests are 'reliable estimates of how programme strategies will work', say Kirban and Jackson (1990). They warn of the danger of operating by instinct instead of employing creative and artistic decisions based on research. A generation ago, Professor William Ehling (1985) warned that public relations would be incomplete and flawed with technician behaviour replacing management-level functioning if it were not based on research. The last word in this section goes to him. He said that public relations is 'a decision-making, problem-solving activity essentially concerned with selecting and specifying end states (goals, objectives) to be attained by an organization or group and with developing, programming and implementing efficient and effective means (courses of action, strategies) for attaining or accomplishing the desired end states'.

THE MEXICAN STATEMENT

In 1978, the Mexican statement, emanating from an international meeting of the same year, states that public relations is the art and social science of analysing trends, predicting their consequences, counselling organization leaders and implementing planned programmes of action which serve both the organization's and the public's interests.

The key words in the original IPR definition are 'planned', 'mutual' and 'publics', whereas in the Mexican statement key words are 'research', 'analysing', 'counselling' and 'both'. The first definition stresses the need to plan public relations and that it should not be a one-way process. It also recognizes, through the plural word 'publics', that organizations have more than one public.

The Mexican definition stresses that work has to be done before any planning can take place. In other words, it excludes knee-jerk reactions to environmental influences and indicates that public relations involves an advisory function. Public relations professionals, whether in-house or outsourced, give advice to senior managers in organizations and emphasize the need to serve the public interest, even where that term is ill-defined.

FROM NEGATIVE TO POSITIVE

It is essential to distinguish corporate public relations from propaganda, which is a deliberate attempt to distort or mislead the public. In order to succeed, public relations must be free from bias and demonstrate a two-way dynamic process where the aim is mutual understanding of the facts even if there is no subsequent agreement on policy or ideology. Organizations often need to respond to unfavourable criticism. In this case, Jefkins (1993) argues for an anatomy of public relations based on the transfer process which shows an organization converting four negative states into positive ones. Thus hostility is converted into sympathy, prejudice to acceptance, apathy to interest and ignorance to knowledge.

SUMMARY

This chapter explains how public relations strategy can be viewed in the light of corporate decision making, environmental scanning, conflict management and organizational culture. The implications and difficulties for the public relations practitioner of short-term (business objectives) and longer-term (corporate mission) accountability are addressed via the benefits of intellectual capital management and alliance networking. These and other approaches allow for greater synthesis between dominant coalitions within an organization and a culture in which strategic public relations as 'extraordinary' management leads to sound performance and ethical control as measures of excellence.

CASE STUDY: SUNCORP-METWAY FINANCE COMPANY, AUSTRALIA

Published by kind permission of IPRA.

Introduction

In 1998, the Queensland Government of Australia decided to sell its 45 per cent share of Suncorp-Metway bank and hired a public relations agency to develop and implement an investment strategy to ensure it wasn't undersubscribed. The Treasury Department had a number of conflicting interests which had to be accommodated by its decision to sell:

● The campaign raised short-term confidence in the share price and helped avoid longer-term vulnerability.
● It used a variety of public relations tools and techniques for environmental scanning, conflict management and political interests.
● It had a value-added role in terms of public education.
● It played a strategic role in communicating to a wide variety of stakeholders who had conflicting demands.

SUNCORP-METWAY

The problem

The company

In September 1998, the Queensland Government's Treasury Department, Queensland Treasury, decided to sell its 45 per cent shareholding in Queensland's largest financial institution, Suncorp-Metway, through an Initial Public Offer. The nature of the government's holding meant that the offer would be Exchanging Instalment Notes that paid interest for the first three years, converting to shares after this period. The offer was one of the ten largest ever conducted in Australia, raising over $1 billion.

The merger of the building society (Suncorp, bank (Metway Bank) and rural lender (QIDC) had occurred 18 months earlier amid market scepticism and political opposition. As such, the decision to sell down the government's remaining holding in the merged group was expected to be controversial and it was perceived that this could leave the group vulnerable to takeover.

Specific problem or opportunity

The Philips Group's consultancy brief was to develop and implement an investment strategy to communicate the details of the offer to investors, ensuring that the issue was fully subscribed. Given the complexities of the political and investment issues impacting on the potential success of the offer, the strategy had to be comprehensive and 'owned' by all members of the investment committee, which was made up of members of Treasury, the underwriters, and legal and ministerial advisers.

The nature of the offer and the capital structure of Suncorp-Metway were both complex. Exchanging Instalment Notes were an unfamiliar concept for many investors confused by the debt and equity character-istics of the notes. In addition, Suncorp-Metway had six different types of shares and notes in its capital structure and, as a result, a variety of shareholders with different rights. The communication programme had to clarify the ability of these different shareholder groups to participate in the new offer, as well as explain the rights attached to the issue of the Exchanging Instalment Notes. The communication also had to be simple enough to encourage other Queensland residents to view the offer as a suitable investment opportunity.

The consultancy's communication strategy considered the communi-cation needs of each stakeholder group, addressed the complexity of the offer, managed issues, marketed the notes, direct mailed one million potential investors, and achieved full subscription for the $1 billion public offer – all within a four-week time frame.

Geographical area

The investment marketing programme developed was targeted primarily at Queensland residents, with a secondary focus on the national investment market. The Queensland Government wanted to be seen to be giving preference to the state's citizens, whilst ensuring that the offer was fully subscribed through national participation.

Research

Prior to the government selling down its remaining shareholding in Suncorp-Metway, the agency had worked with Queensland Treasury to announce the proposal to merge Suncorp, QIDC and Metway Bank, and on the subsequent communication with Metway shareholders in October 1996, who accepted the merger. As a result, the firm had access to valuable resources. However, additional research included:

● media analysis;
● a review of all issues and the development of an issues matrix;

- a performance analysis of Suncorp-Metway, based on broker reports, annual results and share-price fluctuations;
- extensive stakeholder analysis; and
- research into political comment regarding the group made since the announcement to merge the three organizations was made in June 1996.

Planning

Statement of the programme's objectives and measurable criteria

The overall goal of the investment marketing strategy was to support the underwriters in ensuring that the offer was fully subscribed. Measurable objectives included:

- To manage the media, ensuring coverage of the offer followed Queensland Treasury's agenda and that 80 per cent of coverage contained the key messages developed as part of the investment marketing programme.
- To ensure that at least 50 per cent take-up of the offer was from retail investors, primarily from Queensland.
- To manage and contain all issues before they were placed on the political or public agenda. To measure, via media analysis, opposition comment.
- To ensure all communication about the offer was easy to understand prompting a response from the relevant target audiences.

Identification of publics

The programme was targeted at: residents of Queensland; customers and shareholders of Suncorp-Metway; other potential shareholders; financial community; media; Suncorp-Metway staff; government and regulatory authorities, including the Australian Securities and Investment Commission, Australian Stock Exchange and Australian Competition and Consumer Commission.

Formulation of messages

Key messages developed as part of the campaign focused on financial factors of importance to this audience – security, return and potential for capital gain. The complex nature of the security on offer was made simple by comparing its features with other financial products more familiar to the residents of Queensland. The debt characteristics of the notes were compared to fixed-term bank deposits, while the equity features were compared to ordinary shares.

Selection of communication channels

The communication strategy used the call centre, advertising and direct mail as the main communication channels through which to distribute the key messages. These channels were chosen because they would communicate the messages to a vast audience in the short four-week time frame.

Creation of vehicles to carry the message

Communication vehicles to carry the key messages included the Offer Document, media releases, regional and national press and TV advertising, and the call centre. Point of sale posters reinforced the messages in Suncorp-Metway branches, and all shareholder and customer communication distributed by the group during the offer period incorporated the key messages. The call centre script was tailored to ensure that messages were easy to understand and to follow up all other communication materials distributed.

Action taken to consult with management

The Treasurer and Queensland Treasury accepted the consultants' approach of using the commercial reality of the offer as the basis of the investment marketing programme. To ensure their ongoing support for the consultants' programme and the changes implemented as part of the issues management programme, the consultancy firm initiated weekly issues meetings involving the Treasurer's Office, the Assistant Under Treasurer and representatives from the three joint lead managers who were underwriting the offer.

Implementation

Description of the plan's implementation

To achieve the project's goal of supporting the underwriters in ensuring that the offer was fully subscribed, the consultants' strategy was to position the offer as an opportunity for 'mum and dad' investors to 'participate in the success' of Queensland's largest financial institution, Suncorp-Metway.

Investment marketing

The investment campaign included an offer document, direct mail, advertising, branch promotions and a dedicated call centre.

The key marketing tool was the offer document. It had to appeal to Queensland residents, Suncorp-Metway customers, shareholders and members of the general public. Within a three-week period the

Philips Group designed, edited, typeset and produced one million copies of the two-colour, 46-page document and organized the logistics for the distribution of these copies to destinations throughout Australia.

The advertising plan utilized a mix of television and print advertisements to stimulate the target audience to 'get a share' in Suncorp-Metway and benefit from the return, past and future success. The advertisements were designed to generate consumer response by directing potential investors to the call centre toll-free number, their local Suncorp-Metway branch or their investment adviser. The advertisements also built on the existing brand personalities of Suncorp, QIDC and Metway Bank.

A professional call centre staffed between 8.00 am and 10.00 pm supported these marketing activities, seven days a week during the four-week offer period. This service ensured that all queries were answered and all potential investors supplied with a copy of the offer document.

Media programme

The media was utilized to highlight the investment benefits of the issue to the retail market, generating support for the issue with 'mum and dad' investors and residents of Queensland. National, metropolitan and local media reports promoted the positive commercial reality of the issue and generated strong support for the offer.

By the end of the third week of the offer period the Philips Group had generated extensive media courage. To avoid maintaining the offer's place on the media agenda and potentially attracting comment from parties opposed to the sell-down, it was recommended that media relations be scaled down and other marketing tools used to promote the offer. This strategy was successful in containing issues.

Issues management programme

An issues document was developed for each member of the investment committee, outlining potential issues, positioning statements, and questions and answers. In addition, an issues database was established which documented all potential issues, public comment and media reports. This database was reviewed on a daily basis.

Adjustments to the plan

Political issues, call centre feedback and the take-up rate of the offer were monitored daily to ensure that the investment marketing strategy remained relevant and targeted and to minimize any potential issues. The following adjustments were made to the initial plan:

- Call centre staff were tripled in the first two weeks and then altered daily to cope with the call fluctuations resulting from the advertising campaign.
- The advertising programme was revised at various periods throughout the four-week offer period. The advertisement schedule was reduced to cater for the unexpected interest in the offer, and additional advertisements were created to explain the allocation process.
- The media programme was also scaled back to reduce promotion of the offer.

Difficulties encountered

The main limitation of the project was the timeframe in which the investment strategy had to be developed and implemented. The Philips Group had only four weeks to prepare for the $1 billion offer and a four-week offer period in which to implement the project, which included editing and producing one million offer documents.

Several other challenges were successfully overcome during the project:

- The complex nature of the notes was explained in simple terms and the product was compared to other, more familiar investment opportunities where necessary.
- The volatile market, which could have discouraged investors, was used as a selling point given the secure nature of the notes during the first three years when a guaranteed interest payment was paid.
- The potential political debate was controlled through a strong issues management and media programme which set the agenda, rather than responding to it.
- The overwhelming demand for the notes impacted on operations at the call centre and at Suncorp-Metway branches. These issues were dealt with on a daily, and sometimes hourly, basis.

Evaluation

Investment marketing

The offer, which raised $1.012 billion, closed 2.5 times oversubscribed with more than 60 per cent of the available notes going to 'mum and dad' investors. As part of the offer, preference was given to Queenslanders as well as existing Suncorp-Metway shareholders and EIN Series 1 Note Holders.

More than 221,000 eligible applications were received, with almost 72 per cent of those from Queensland. Every eligible applicant received an allocation.

Media programme

The results of the media relations programme are summarized as:

- 128 positive press stories out of a total 138;
- 31 positive feature articles out of a total 35;
- 18 positive television grabs and 60 radio interviews;
- 89.6 per cent of stories contained key messages drafted by the Philips Group and Queensland Treasury.

In all instances the consultancy's key messages were used and after 8 October, when the decision was made to cease proactive generation of stories, the media followed their lead with only four stories appearing between 9 October and the closure of the offer on 6 November.

Political programme

During the offer period, no political debate was generated in or out of Parliament by the Opposition. The Opposition spokesman's comments accounted for fewer than 13 out of 173 media reports, despite the sell-down being against the Conservative agenda. By controlling the flow and quality of information being disseminated about the sell-down, the Philips Group contained any issues or political positioning by the government's opposition.

Reaching stakeholders

More than 1.1 million copies of the offer document were distributed to households during the offer period. Of the 54,620 calls recorded at the call centre, 36,503 were requests for additional copies of the prospectus.

The majority of feedback received from investors at the call centre included comments on the appeal of the offer document and the ease of completing the application forms.

3

Image in a 'celebrity' society: public relations strategy as integrated communication

Public relations practitioners are often confused and bemused by the links between corporate image, corporate identity and reputation, but it is clear that the accumulation of empirical research on corporate image formation has led to the corporate identity literature of today. The *Collins English Dictionary* on current English usage offers the following definitions:

Image – A mental picture; idea produced by the imagination or personality presented to the public by a person, organization, etc.
Identity – The state of having unique identifying characteristics or the individual characteristics by which a person or thing is recognized.

Reputation – Notoriety or fame, especially for some specified characteristic. While repute is the public estimation of a person or thing to be as specified, usually passive.

Stuart (1999) believes that corporate identity models, by including variables of organizational culture, corporate strategy, corporate communication and integrated communication, provide a more definitive model of the management process itself.

IMAGE

Image has had a bad press in public relations terms yet image consultants continue to be in great demand. There are a number of reasons for this. The technological era has made people every-where aware of, if not educated about, the roles of government and big business in society, and organizations have become sensi-tive to the fact that corporate image operates in different dimen-sions for different audiences, to arrive as close as possible to what Boorstin (1963) describes as pseudo-ideal, which must be synthetic, believable, passive, vivid and ambiguous. Part of the bad press may lie in the fact that image can be as abstract a concept as Boorstin suggests and therefore lays itself open to suspicion. Bernstein (1991) calls it a vaporous concept of imprecise language, superficial thinking and self-styled image makers who contribute to the insubstantiality. However, Mackiewicz (1993) believes that a strong corporate image is an essential asset in today's era of borderless competition and argues so what? However nebulous, image is reality because people can only react to what they experi-ence and perceive. Carl Rogers (1993) said, 'I do not react to some abstract reality but to my perception of this reality. It is this percep-tion which for me is reality.'

Thus the nature of corporate image itself, however unpalatable, remains a growth area of public relations productivity which, in combination with a growing body of knowledge about stake-holder expectation, remains a popular focus of interest. Even companies that prefer to adopt a low profile are assessing their corporate image and its significance when studying their stake-holders' perceptions of their company policies, procedures and behaviour. Other writers find that the low profile most usually associated with such companies evokes words such as avoidance, uninvolved, passive, yielding and uninfluential, and companies may spend as much time and money on maintaining their low profile as they could maintaining a higher profile.

Belief systems play a part in people's attitudes. Unfavourable beliefs can lead to a drop in sales or a lowering of share price which will have to be corrected by public relations involvement. Many writers and practitioners argue that beliefs make up product and brand images and that people act on those images. The checks and balances in any strategic campaign allow for modification of organizational behaviour or public perception to adjust knowledge, feelings or belief accordingly. Writing during the same period, Eiser suggested that a situation in which there is no communication loop between individuals' expressed attitudes and their behaviour will lead to a situation where stakeholders can only communicate their preferences through actions rather than words.

More current studies show that image does not consist of a single reality held by individuals, but that they hold a series of linked pictures consisting of many elements or objects which merge together and which are interpreted through language. Lynch (1991) considers graphic representation to be an appropriate measure of city image whereas Bernstein might prefer verbal descriptions of companies and industries based on images formed through conversation and written reports.

Image and branding

Corporate image in the professional public relations sense goes back to the 1950s with the introduction of new commercial television stations. Marketing firms jumped on the bandwagon of creating brand image without any systematic theoretical foundation, so that people like Newman (1956) reported that 'the business firm may have no body to be kicked but it does have a character' and Boulding (1956) said, 'the relationship between corporate image and the behaviour of the consumers, saying that what the individual, especially a celebrity on television, believed to be true, was true for him'.

When advertisers picked up the notion of image as a tool for branding products as well as corporate identity, writers of the day like Mayer (1961) saw the brand as a visible status symbol, but 30 years later Gorb (1992) was to argue that the business of corporate image design had become trivialized by too close association with external visual symbolism like logos. He recognized that the dynamics of image lie within the firm itself and have as much to do with manners and interrelationships as with markets. Bernstein's view is that the image can be built into a product, whereas it can at best only be adjusted for a company, whereas Macrae (1991) believes that a corporate brand can be translated into a mission of pride for staff in the pursuit of excellence, advancing company reputation among stakeholders. From this a branded corporate image can grow into reality.

With the derogatory representation of image as being artificial, the work of O'Sullivan *et al* (1994) was seminal in that it approached the subject of image in terms of its original meaning as being a visual representation of reality, which is important in understanding the world around us, whether employee or shareholder of a company.

An interesting case in point is the British retail conglomerate, Marks & Spencer plc, whose corporate image design had hardly become what Gorb called 'trivialized' and whose dynamics within the firm had more to do with manners and interrelationships than markets. Nevertheless, they currently have to rework their existing image if they are to evolve and adapt changes to meet their corporate values while meeting the expectations of their stakeholders, especially their customers who have deserted them. Thus Mackiewicz's definition of corporate image as 'the perceived sum of the entire organization, its plans and objectives' is very relevant to this case. By arguing that corporate image encompasses the company's products, services, management style, corporate communication and actions around the world, he could be describing any organization in crisis where the positive sum of these perceptual components must be re-evaluated to give the company back the market advantages it once enjoyed or to increase market share and investor popularity. A neutral corporate image can develop over time to become what Boorstin would describe as so impartial that it repels nobody. Indeed, Kotler (1988) suggests that corporate image can be highly specific or highly diffused and that some organizations may not want or need a very specific image. Some organizations prefer a diffused image so that different groups can project their needs into this organization, and this has clearly taken place in the British people's psyche.

IDENTITY

Given that there is a clear correlation between business and policy and corporate image in terms of corporate strategy, perhaps the first question the strategist must ask is, 'What business are we now in?' before asking the question, 'What is our identity to ourselves and others?' If an organization is unclear about its identity, then it will not be able to assess its image as perceived by the different stakeholders, nor how these perceptions should be prioritized in terms of strategic planning, policy and practice. For any business strategy to be effective, it must be comprehended accurately by the target publics, or at least in the way that the corporate vision and mission determine.

Mind over matter

The research, monitoring and evaluation of corporate image and identity is a complex psychological and behavioural activity. The company message must reach many different stakeholders on many different subjects while retaining a core image, even though those stakeholders' expectations are different. In making what O'Sullivan *et al* called the visual representation of reality, corporate image, based on clear identity, must be made tangible and quantifiable. Only then is it possible to realize competitive advantage.

Superficiality vs substance

Dowling (1993) suggested that in measuring corporate image and culture held by staff, the effects of mass communication achieved through advertising and corporate identity programmes and the changing customers' perceptions of the company must be taken into account. If change is desired, rigorous control is essential. If the wrong variables are changed or the sequence of change is wrong, the results can be costly failure. A company's communication strategy should cover every aspect of an organization that its stakeholders are or should be aware of. John Stanley (1991) argued that no organization can fool its stakeholders with hype. Corporate communication is only effective if it conveys a message of strength and substance as well as its corporate values.

Globalization

In the era of global communications, corporate values have come to the fore. The Internet has made debates on social responsibility and accountability a new type of challenge for corporate image campaigning. Ethical issues can arise from any part of an organization's business activity and thus form part of the core business operation. There is hardly one aspect of public relations or corporate communication that can avoid addressing corporate identity, whether in terms of the letter of the law or the spirit of sound corporate citizenship. It is increasingly recognized that the value of ethics statements goes beyond the interest of employee stakeholder groups to embrace all other stakeholders, if not society as a whole, that add value to an organization. Houlden (1988) recognized that being proactive about the way society views their company is a key skill for modern-day organizational leaders if corporate image is not to be damaged. Singer (1993) calls this 'consequentialism', meaning that ethical judgement goes beyond individual likes and dislikes to produce social mores and norms which form the core of any corporate value system, no matter where or how the company operates.

REPUTATION

Nowhere has the issue of measurement methods in practice been more debated than in the area of American multinational companies and the reputations that they attract. The readers of the journal *Fortune* are asked to rate the largest companies in their own commercial sector on eight key factors using a scale of 0–10 as follows:

Quality of management
Quality of products or services
Financial soundness
Ability to attract, develop and keep talented people
Use of corporate assets
Value as long-term investment
Innovativeness
Community and environmental responsibility.

This particular technique, called the Fortune Corporate Reputation Index, and other measures such as Britain's Financial Times/PricewaterhouseCoopers Seven Factor Model of Business Performance have been criticized by Van Riel (1995), drawing on the criticisms of Maathuis (1993) plus Fryxell and Wang (1994), who argues that, although these surveys are based on the opinions of so-called experts, 'it is likely that different results would be obtained were the same measurement instrument to be used by a different group'. Further, 'as a consequence, reputation scores as evaluated by the *Fortune* respondents, relate more directly to reputation as a measure of an investment'. Van Riel fails to make a positive correlation between the concepts of image, identity and reputation in measurable terms and appears in places to use the words interchangeably. His comment about applied image research and the various methods in frequent use warns practitioners that the quality of research is determined not only by the methods used but also by the quality of the questions formulated. The degree of detail in the question determines the degree of possible refinement in the answer, he argues, and states that 'if a company requires further information about its reputation, then it must embark upon research in greater depth'.

This inevitably has implications for the selection of consultants who in the main are seen to be more objective about assessing the reputation of an organization and therefore more usually given the research task.

Ewing *et al* (1999) argue that research is more thorough if the consulting firm has no prior connection to the company and is totally unfamiliar to the client. In such instances the client is likely to get more people involved in the selection process. Also, consulting firms with international links are favoured not only by clients who have interests in overseas projects but also by those who actually participate in large domestic projects. 'Firms that have foreign partnerships are preferred over the local ones because they are deemed to have the international expertise to offer clients better services in the long run.' Their study also reveals that reputation is not a measure of risk and that 'both factors are separate constructs altogether'. Ewing *et al* found that, if a company does not think or recognize that it has a problem, it will be suspicious of an outsider who tells it that it does have a problem and become more cautious of unsolicited advice. In today's climate of corporate account-ability, no organization can afford to take such an arrogant or complacent view of communication nor fail to address its strategic implications.

SUMMARY

The success of any public relations campaign at corporate level depends on its philosophy and mission with regard to the wider community and society as a whole. To that end, public relations strategies usually contain a remit to research, monitor, maintain and evaluate public perception of the organization as a whole in terms of its image, identity and reputation.

CASE STUDY: KRAFT JACOBS SUCHARD, ROMANIA

Published by kind permission of IPRA.

Introduction

This firm exceeded its objective in becoming 'leader' of the Romanian confectionery market and came second in Central and Eastern Europe in total product sales volume. This was achieved by concentrating on its image by sponsoring a national child nutrition programme between 1998 and 2000.

Key points

The company:

- involved a wide range of community groups and public bodies in its educational endeavours and thus developed a clear identity in Romania;
- engaged experts in the field to speak on behalf of the company and established a clear identity;
- enjoyed a high media profile for enhanced reputation, especially through its work with children and their parents.

KRAFT JACOBS SUCHARD

The problem

Kraft Jacobs Suchard's stated philosophy is to bring real benefits to communities where the company is present, in fields like education, nutrition, environment protection and culture.

Living conditions in Romania are poor and this affects the nation's health. Statistics show that two-thirds of Romanian children have anaemia, and in fact half of the Romanian population considered to be healthy has diet problems.

The publication of the United Nations Development Programme (UNDP) study on the aggravation of the Romanian population's state of health had a strong influence on Prais Corporate Communications, which led to the consultants' decision to initiate in Romania, on behalf of Kraft Jacobs Suchard Romania, a pilot educational programme on nutrition issues.

When selecting the programme addressees, they considered the most vulnerable groups of the population – children and future mothers. The Romanian school system does not include at the level of I–IV grade classes information related to adequate nutrition or food and personal hygiene. Also, due to the lack of financial resources of the Romanian medical system, the physicians are not able to provide documentation to future or young mothers regarding their nutrition during pregnancy, as well as the children's feeding supervision.

These are the two directions on which the consultants developed the public relations pilot educational programme on nutrition, called 'Infant Nutrition – Essence of a Generation's Health'. The programme was implemented in two major communities: Bucharest and Brasov, the town in which Kraft Jacobs Suchard Romania is located, with extension at national level.

Research

Before planning the programme development, the public relations team performed a large amount of research, gathering data at national level to identify the programme target categories and the most efficient tools in communicating the message and achieving the objectives. The research was based on the data of UNDP surveys, statistics of the Institute for Research of Life Quality, as well as on the scientific documentation provided by the specialists of the Romanian Institute of Nutrition and Metabolic Diseases.

A team of Prais Corporate Communication consultants and medical specialists processed the data and analysed the influence of economic factors on the nutrition and health status of the Romanian population. The results of the analysis demonstrated that a public relations community programme would be more efficient if addressed to the most vulnerable groups: children and future mothers.

Planning

The public relations pilot educational programme was developed from May to December 1998 and was also planned to continue during the school year 1999–2000.

The objectives of the public relations programme were target oriented to:

- develop an educational campaign for children and future mothers in the communities of Bucharest and Brasov, with extension at national level;
- influence the public bodies through the educational campaign on healthy nutrition;
- launch a national civic debate on the necessity of educating people on rational nutrition and changing mentality for raising the quality of life.

The public relations programme aimed to mobilize local communities and families to be the message forwarders and to raise public awareness on the utility and necessity of such educational programmes, state-financed. The communication channels were selected according to programme objectives, to find the best approach to initiate the mass media debate. Therefore, the public relations team consulted the representatives of the Ministry of Health, the Ministry of Education and the Institute for the Mother and Child Caring, and challenged specialists of the Institute of Nutrition and Metabolic Diseases, physicians and students in a voluntary effort.

A joint team, comprising the board of Kraft Jacobs Suchard Romania and the public relations consultants, together with specialists of the Institute of Nutrition and Metabolic Diseases, formulated the messages to be communicated, depending on the category addressed. Owing to his involvement and experience in the nutrition field, the opinion leader was nominated to be Professor Constantin Ionescu Tirgoviste, the general director of the Institute of Nutrition and Metabolic Diseases, and a specialist with a worldwide reputation.

Reports on the programme status and results, as well as monthly schedules, were submitted to the Kraft Jacobs Suchard Romania board, which was permanently connected to the public relations team. The bilateral analysis of the achievements ensured ongoing programme adjustment according to the reaction of the target audiences. The results of the public relations programme were measured through the number of people involved, their responsiveness and appreciation, as well as through the mass media debate related to the health nutrition theme.

Implementation

The first level of the public relations educational programme was addressed to third/fourth grade children, who received information about healthy nutrition. From May to December 1998, pupils of Bucharest and Brasov participated in classes on nutrition and personal and alimentary hygiene.

The public relations programme was developed under the agreement and supervision of the Ministry of Education, the Ministry of Health and the Institute of Nutrition and Metabolic Diseases. The public relations team, together with the specialists from the Institute of Nutrition and Metabolic Diseases, prepared the scientific documentation on nutrition, the basis for the structure of the lessons. The message approach was conceived as friendly, positive and adequate to the children's level of understanding. The lessons were presented in the form of interactive theatre plays associated with games, contests and prizes. A team of medical representatives and students of the Theatre and Film Academy of Bucharest held the classes.

On the second level of the public relations programme, young mothers were addressed in a brochure entitled 'You Eat Healthy, You Have a Healthy Child' (sic!) containing recommendations prescribed by specialists at the Institute of Nutrition and Metabolic Diseases. More than 1,500 brochures were distributed free of charge to nine medical institutions – hospital maternity and polyclinics from Brasov and Bucharest, and as many young mothers benefited from medical advice. Seminars, where physicians held lectures, were also organized on this occasion.

The events and achievements of the public relations educational programme on the two levels of action were permanently promoted in the mass media at national level.

The analysis of the 1998 achievements showed the necessity of continuing the public relations educational programme on nutrition. Within the 1999 public relations programme, an educational kit was delivered to more than 5,000 children. The kit contained books for each pupil, called 'Adventures in Nutrition Land', nutrition didactic sheets for teachers and an educational poster.

The 1999 public relations programme concept also comprised the launch of the contest 'When a Child Laughs: Wisdom and Love is at

Play'. This rewarded children's creativity through drawings, poems, stories and theatre play, and commended teachers' educational results.

Evaluation

The results of the public relations programme, as measured by teachers' and doctors' answers to evaluation questionnaires, indicated the largest-ever participation of children in any educational programme and some of the strongest media coverage ever recorded for such a programme. The questionnaire, which was completed by the teachers and school directors involved in the educational programme, revealed that all subjects considered the project as necessary and of great importance for the community. Marks of 'very good' and 'exceptional' given by teachers on the questionnaire illustrated the appreciation felt and the success of the programme.

The children's responsiveness to the nutrition classes was the most satisfying result of the public relations educational programme. It resulted in a great number of drawings, stories, poems and theatre plays created as a result of their participation.

Research done by the public relations team on the results of the public relations brochure 'You Eat Healthy, You Have a Healthy Child' revealed that doctors and mothers appreciated the initiative and all target audiences requested the continuation of the project.

In a general approach, this public relations programme led to the onset of a public debate in the mass media on the subject of the health status of Romanian children and future mothers, as the analysis of the mass media coverage showed. From May to December 1998, the programme generated 44 written press materials, of which 55 per cent were accompanied by visual elements. The titles of two-thirds of the articles referred to aspects of community interest. Scientific information, specialists' opinion and health-related issues appear in 31 articles, while the public relations educational programme is generally presented in 28 articles. The audio-visual media generated 37 materials broadcast by radio (17) and TV (20) stations in the country.

An overview of the media coverage of the public relations pilot programme, as well as the target audiences' responsiveness, shows that the educational programme, as an expression of an active involvement in a sensitive Romanian community problem, had been very well received.

4

Employees as ambassadors: public relations strategy in an HR context

EMPLOYEES AND TWO-WAY COMMUNICATION

The flexibility required of people in organizations has brought about a re-emergence of the importance of the central role of employee relations based on symmetrical communication. This includes what used to be called participative management.

The important issues for in-house public relations specialists can be addressed by understanding the strategic models and thinking from human resource management. Few HR models move from rhetoric or ideology to the reality of the workplace without the intervention of expert communicators. In Chapter 2 we asked what business the organization was in so as to articulate its mission as a basis for strategic planning. In-house specialists need to ensure that they have enough authority and influence to ensure that strategic plans and policies work through from the CEO to individuals at all levels of the organization. The PR Director, working alongside the CEO and being fully conversant with the organization's culture and value system, is able to identify any changes required to that system for the mission to be achieved. Having sight of the strategic plan, the public relations team assesses the implications of the plan for public relations structure, process and resources. An appraisal of the tools and techniques required to motivate staff, retain key skills and ensure competency for enhanced productivity, performance and commitment through IT, newsletters, reward, skilfully targeted messages and other techniques is a normal part of such assessment. The principal strategic HR theories, models, plans and policies are complementary to those of public relations and often require senior public relations managers to work closely with senior HR managers, especially in areas such as employee relations and collective bargaining disputes.

With the increase in virtual organization and the imperative to link employees in distant parts of a global organization, the need to control from the centre requires sensitive and expert handling if it is not to corrupt the values upon which most organizations in the west rely. In cultural terms, the corporate communication system becomes part of the core corporate business strategy binding the organization together.

Yet it is interesting to see how few academic texts on human resource strategies include communication as a key competency. Strategic HR planning, policy making and practice tend to be debated around recruitment and selection, performance appraisal, assessment compensation, training and development, succession and career profiling, job design and evaluation. These are cited as being essential support activities for operationalizing corporate strategy, but HR frequently fails to identify the contribution of communication for the resources necessary to cope with the demands of constant change. An experienced public relations practitioner could argue that this is why so many large-scale change programmes fail, including business process re-engineering and total quality management programmes. The role of public relations in helping organizations to change and to sustain new behaviours is always underestimated.

Many key competencies for integrated human resource management strategy parallel key areas in which public relations generally has been in demand. Both specialists may share sound leadership through the application of a clear organizational mission; competent managing of people, skills, abilities and knowledge through the gathering of intellectual capital; monitoring and measuring information to ensure that work groups identify with and 'own' the information best suited to their function and accomplishment of the mission; and maintenance of a culture that contributes to an open system in which people feel they are able to say what they feel if it is in the best interests of their responsibilities and can offer potential for growth and development.

INTERNAL COMMUNICATION

Thus, large-scale change internal communication programmes must consider the following:

- They must address short-term critical issues faced and understood by managers and not start with global and long-term business communication programmes published as documents which are insensitive to the needs of individuals.
- They must create a realistic view of what can be achieved and not rely too heavily on raising expectations.
- They must offer opportunity for behavioural learning rather than representational learning, that is, change what people do rather than encourage learning through the use of new words and language alone to discourage the tension between what people say and what people do.
- There should be devolved involvement of managers at the sharp end instead of creating top-heavy and exclusive project teams which drive programmes without consultation and therefore with inadequate research.
- They must be open to changing environmental pressures and priorities.
- They must include even the short-term pragmatists and the long-term cynics who refuse to engage emotionally.

A study of the 1994 signal workers' dispute in British Rail by

Crossman and McIlwee (1995) identified nine key areas in which public relations could have played an important role. These were the political forces, the economic forces, the cultural forces, the mission and strategy, the organization structure, the way human resources were managed in terms of flexibility, quality, commitment and strategic integration, the stakeholders' interests, and the community relations and union relations. The Railtrack case study at the end of this chapter offers a further example.

Mintzberg's model (1994) also speaks to the in-house PRO. He offers five definitions of strategy, all of which have some degree of interrelationship. They are strategy as plan, strategy as ploy, strategy as pattern, strategy as position, strategy as perspective. Today's generic models of strategy highlight four approaches, namely classical ('analyse, plan and command'), evolutionary ('keeping costs low and options open'), processual ('playing by the local rules') and systemic, all of which shadow the history of public relations, from classical through evolutionary and processual to the systemic model espoused in this book and others.

These four dimensions include variables of power and culture, which many of the traditional models lacked. Inevitably, this is important in assessing the nature of organizational reality. For example, there would be a different emphasis on an organization driven by its investment stakeholders such as financiers, compared with an organization driven more by the community and local government or the market and suppliers.

COPING WITH THE FLEXIBLE FIRM

Like all functions within an organization, PR has as its main aim the corporate objectives. Key writers in this area are Fombrun, Sisson and Timperley, Miles and Snow, Beer, Guest, Schule and Jackson and Miller, but perhaps the most familiar name to public relations specialists is Atkinson with his 'flexible firm' model. This British model proposed that employers seek an optimal balance between functional, numerical and financial forms of flexibility through segmenting the labour force into core and peripheral groups. The corporate message must be consistent but may have to be transmitted in different ways to these different groups, whether they are performing in-house or as outsourced labour, such as associates or consultants.

Although the concept of change took root fairly readily with writers such as Rosabeth Moss-Kanter, Barry Stein and Todd Jick, the proliferation of models that followed has sometimes assumed that all organizations are being affected by change to the same degree and in the same way because of new technology and the fall-out following the long period of global economic depression. This is patently not the case, but clearly the larger the organization, the larger the change needed to alter character and performance given organizational complexity. As stated in Chapter 2, the key is the way that decisions are made. Fineman and Mangham suggest that there are four approaches that can be taken – a structural approach, a human resource approach, a political approach and a symbolic approach, the latter seeing change as a process of developing myths, metaphors, rituals and ceremonies to cope with the uncertainty and ambiguity that planning and control measures cannot cope with. It is important that the public relations planner is aware of which approach drives decision making in his or her organization if he or she is to articulate appropriately the meanings in the messages being put across. Whichever is the dominant force, communication is the essential leverage and link for any decision making, given that employees and managers must have participated in the decision-making process if the change is to be 'owned' and thus successfully operationalized.

One of the key areas familiar to public relations consultants will be the development of commitment (based on attitude, behaviour and exchange) as a means of achieving flexibility and change. Exchange theory is seeing revitalized interest because it focuses on concepts of loyalty arising from mutual understanding and benefit. Organizations that demanded total commitment, often at the expense of family and social stability, have come under fire in the recent past and employers are now beginning to realize that there has to be beneficial exchange of one sort or another, material or otherwise, between both parties. Unlike economic exchange, social exchange involves unspecified obligations, the fulfilment of which depends on trust, because it cannot be enforced in the absence of a binding contract. Some organizations have therefore formally introduced the concept of the psychological contract as part of appraisal, whereby transactional contracts are linked to economic exchange but relational obligations or relational contracts are linked to social exchange. The public relations value-added component is measured by levels of morale, performance and productivity, as well as traditional communication audits and suggestion schemes, employee rewards and recognition through awards gained by meeting sales targets and other objectives.

COMMUNICATION IN LEADERSHIP

Of continuing importance for public relations practice is its role and intervention in the management of total quality (TQM). Canadian writer Gareth Morgan looked at practitioner competencies in this area and there is not one of his nine leadership competence modes in which communication does not play a central operational role (Table 4.1).

Table 4.1 *Communication in leadership*

Cultural model	PR model
• Reading the environment	• Environmental scanning (external
• Proactive management	forces), issues management,
• Leadership and vision	planning, monitoring and
• Human resource	evaluation
management	• Mission/intelligence data
• Promoting creativity, learning	• Relationship building/perception
and information	• Adaptive/interpretive strategies
• Skills of remote management	• Media relations, lobbying
• Using information	• Interdisciplinary nature of
technology	PR/crisis management
• Managing complexity	• A management discipline
• Developing contextual	involving a wide variety of
competencies	stakeholder relations

Writers such as Gregerson *et al* (1997) stress the need for competent global leaders compared with other resources. It has been reported that CEOs spend between 50 and 80 per cent of their working hours on average on communicating with stakeholders of one sort or another, which suggests that they not only develop strategy but operationalize it (Table 4.2).

Table 4.2 *Importance of global leadership compared with other needs (based on a survey of US Fortune 500 firms in 1997)*

Dimension	Average rating
Competent global leaders	6.1
Adequate financial resources	5.9
Improved international communication technology	5.1
Higher quality local national workforce	5.0
Greater political stability in developing countries	4.7
Greater national government support of trade	4.5
Lower tariff/trade restrictions in other countries	4.4

1 = Not at all important; 7 = Extremely important

Source: Gregerson *et al* (1997)

The organizational development movement (OD) of the 1970s focused on organizational change through the need to integrate systems and groups, including shared problem solving which demanded higher levels of quality and leadership. The 1990s version of organizational development is about the dynamic links between business decisions, external forces and the organizational consequences. It is here, in the concept of change and the ever-learning organization, that public relations expertise is proving critical and high profile once more.

Along with HR practitioners, public relations practitioners must have in common the concept of performance management that promises or offers a way to link the micro activities of managing individuals and groups to the macro issue of corporate objectives. So how and where does individual communication performance link with strategic management? If we are to use the indicators emerging from the academic press, there are three principal areas which involve communication expertise and behaviour: 1) quality assurance through communication audits, 2) expediting core values as manifested by the mission and ethics statements, and 3) managing new and more democratic systems of worker control through strong leadership and consultation processes based on sound communication processes.

OPERATIONAL PUBLIC RELATIONS PRACTICE

Strategic internal communication, as part of overall public relations strategy, is a dynamic operational process linked to the business plan, for example, through the following professional activities:

- Establish and target internal groups.
- Plan an integrated communication programme.
- Communicate effectively by word and deed.
- Manage strategically around size, geography and international issues at home and overseas.
- Assess the competitive environment.
- Make every employee public relations accountable through understanding and know-how.
- Decide the value and function of all publications.
- Establish fair and just employee communication channels from induction to retirement or redundancy.
- Organize efficient monitoring and management of notice-boards and electronic messaging.
- Maintain suggestion schemes through a rewarding open-communication culture.
- Incorporate crisis management techniques into headquarters record systems, computer networks and common-sense face-to-face briefings.
- Strengthen corporate identity and reputation by providing internal and external information.
- Clarify the relationship and boundaries between external and internal communication, the dual role and the capacity of those responsible to handle the delicate balance.
- Explain policy rules and regulations and be able to talk to people at all levels.
- Monitor attitude through communication audits.
- Evaluate corporate vision regularly with short-term aims.

Corporate strategy is no longer a question of bottom-up or top-down communication. It tries to involve as many people as possible in a common purpose. A strong and influential PRO, backed by a competent team, is the communication conduit for facilitating and delivering meaning and message to a CEO Board. The PRO does this by managing barometers, collating and analysing intellectual capital that feeds critically into organizational decision making. Some of the difficulties for managers in attempting coordination and communication between many functional groups, units or departments are that they have their own professional ties to expertise and standards which may or may not parallel the objectives of the corporate mission. In-house PR practitioners provide a forum for airing barriers to communication and provide the expertise in turning potential functional problems into positive contributions to the communication programme, which is fundamental to an organization's corporate strategy. In the case study that follows, it is possible to see how public relations specialists designed a campaign to increase efficiency and improve morale.

SUMMARY

Employee stakeholder relations relies extensively on sound internal communication and this chapter focuses on the role of public relations in effective change programmes. It takes a number of generic HR strategic models and identifies strategic approaches that parallel PR approaches in the carrying out of professional activities.

CASE STUDY: RAILTRACK PLC, BRITAIN

Published by kind permission of IPRA.

Introduction

The communication strategy at Railtrack came into focus after the company was privatized in 1997. Major revisions were required to it to ensure successful short and long-term change by management and employees at every level.

Key points

- The communication strategy demonstrates the significance of public relations in the change process.

- It reflects the importance of internal scanning to identify key audiences, sub-audiences and tools necessary to ensure that an integrated and coherent approach is maintained.
- It emphasizes the importance of research and evaluation in the symmetrical communication process.
- It shows how public relations strategy is a core component of corporate strategy.

RAILTRACK PLC

The problem

By mid-1997, Railtrack plc, the UK's railway infrastructure company, was emerging from the experience of being floated on the London Stock Market. As it continued to adjust to post-privatization business relationships in an environment of intense public, regulatory and political scrutiny, Railtrack's attention focused on raising performance and the quality of service provided to increasingly vocal customers. In addition, the challenge of ensuring economic fitness following the forthcoming regulatory review in April 2001 was a looming priority.

In 1997 Railtrack publicly stated a commitment to invest £17 billion (raised to £27 billion in 1999), funded through borrowing, in improving the rail infrastructure over the next 10 years. For every £10 million raised, £1 million of profit had to be made to secure the borrowing. Internally, therefore, the imperative was to become far more commercially minded, rather than purely operational. Never before had the employees had to concern themselves with the fundamental economics of a commercial business, and make day-to-day and longer-term decisions based on it. To drive the commercial focus down into the operations would involve a shift from a centralized and hierarchical style to one where decision making and responsibility are devolved as far as possible. The challenge remains to encourage customer focus and operational innovation, whilst achieving the commercial requirement and without sacrificing safety and performance.

Traditionally the company's internal communication (IC) approach was predominantly pastoral and lacked the required strategic and business focus. Internal communication posts were filled on an ad hoc basis and few people had professional backgrounds in professional PR. The challenge for the corporate affairs team was to transform it.

Research

To help them, Railtrack brought in Hedron Consulting Ltd, specialists in internal communication. Its consultants brought a good deal of knowledge and experience of other companies and industries, both within the UK and internationally, from which Railtrack could learn. The brief to Hedron was to work with the existing internal communication team (seven people spread across seven zones in the UK – some part-time) to develop and implement a commercially focused corporate internal communication strategy. In addition, Hedron were to strengthen the head office in-house team, which would spearhead internal communication implementation. The starting premise was that from the experience of other organizations, it was essential to view internal communication as a key part of the management process that can either support or undermine the commercial objectives of the business, rather than a 'nice to do' or a 'feel-good' activity.

To deliver this approach the team had to identify the key business objectives and establish how they related to people's day-to-day job attitudes and behaviours. They did this by analysing the core business and operational plans and reports (some in the public domain, including the annually published Network Management Statement and the Train Operating Company customer satisfaction index) and by interviewing the key members of the board. The highly sensitive internal business plan documentation defined the core business objectives that internal communication was to be tasked with supporting and this was agreed between the research team and top management.

The communication shortfall between what was needed and what existed, the current from 'excellent' communication practice, was assessed. The effectiveness was judged against the role communication can play in supporting the attainment of business objectives by ensuring they are first known and secondly understood. The data analysed included two employee attitude surveys, an internal communication audit and discussions with a broad range of senior HR and line managers, as well as front-line staff.

Planning

IC objectives were articulated as:

1. ensure that all staff understand business objective priorities and their drivers, and their relevance to the successful future of the company and the railway;
2. help employees understand the business objectives, and ensure that employees are clear about their role and contribution to their achievement;
3. encourage/ensure that managers and staff enter frequently into dialogue about performance: potential enhancements, barriers, resources, processes;

4. provide the processes and training whereby information can be more easily accessed and rapidly transferred around the organization to support efficient working practices.

The strategy was to modernize the basic internal communication approaches throughout the company so that they placed greater emphasis on dialogue about the business. The content of communication was to be re-balanced to give a greater 'share of voice' to strategic, operational and educational information about the business.

The concept of communication 'rights' and 'responsibilities' of management and staff was introduced, to change the way in which communication was viewed, talked about and used inside the business. This is fundamental to developing a culture where it is no longer acceptable either for employees to be kept in the dark about the business's commercial priorities, or for them to say they do not need to know.

Critical success factors were identified. The most challenging was to ensure that senior managers placed as much value on internal communication as on external communication. They viewed internal communication as a way to inform staff about the management process as well as to enable staff to make commercially minded judgements.

Implementation

At the end of October 1997, Gerald Corbett, the chief executive, signed off seven core 'actions' with a budget of £730,000. Combined, these actions created a new framework for communication, introduced the strategic communication objectives and repositioned internal communication in Railtrack.

Action One

First, external candidate Ken Hunter was appointed Head of Internal Communication, to lead an HQ and zonal team and spearhead the transformation. This was important in raising the profile of communication as a means of motivating employees and improving performance.

The first 'action' was to ensure that information could reach all employees at work within 24 hours (previously only 65 per cent), rather than the two weeks it could take for information to reach out-based employees. This was crippling the organization's ability to deal with crucial issues and to communicate rapidly with employees on industrial relations. By providing additional basic technology (phones/faxes) the reach went up to nearer 95 per cent – on-duty staff having access to information within four hours of issue. The results were significant. The board acknowledged the pivotal contribution it made in reversing an

RMT strike call, which succeeded with other railway companies. The board was able to have information in front of employees well before any trade union material was issued. It was able to explain why the RMT demands were untenable. Employees understood the logic and voted not to strike.

Action Two

The second 'action' significantly enhanced the opportunity for staff to engage in dialogue about the business with their senior management. A radical programme of regional 'railshows' led by the CEO and zone directors saw over 25 per cent of staff of all levels discussing the strategic direction of the business and how it related to people's day-to-day jobs. The outcomes were strong:

- 91 per cent felt as a result that they could link their objectives to those of their zone and the company;
- 84 per cent said they had a better of understanding of where they could contribute to the work of the zone;
- 85 per cent had confidence in the future of Railtrack.

Those not present received the core information and points from discussion using the new media.

Action Three

The third 'action' undertook a fundamental review of internal media and created a framework of media which enabled employees to share learning and best practice, as well as provide the knowledge and context to understand why and how decisions were made. Already these framework media have made a substantial return through the volume and quality of best practice sharing and cost saving ideas they have facilitated. One article alone earned £100,000 by highlighting to the European Affairs team a project eligible for funding. Without the publication this would have been missed.

Action Four

The fourth 'action' revised the team briefing process to catalyse dialogue about the business at team level. To overcome the hierarchical and cultural weaknesses of the existing team-briefing process, a radical approach was taken. *Teamtalk* was piloted, amended and rolled out across the country. Written in prose by the CEO or respective zone director, *teamtalk* focuses only on strategic business information. It complements, not replaces, line-specific briefings. It goes to all employees in a zone at the same time, in advance of the team meeting at which its meaning at local level is discussed. It can stand alone for more isolated members of staff. Questions are asked of employees who can respond either as a team or as individuals. So far, feedback and focus groups have shown that *teamtalk* is well received among many and is prompting dialogue about the business. However, senior managers have not responded quickly enough, which has discouraged people. Senior managers have been criticized for not being controversial enough and refusing to acknowledge mistakes. They have been challenged by the internal communication team to address these criticisms.

Actions Five, Six and Seven

The other three core 'actions' were to revise the senior management communication meeting, so it role-models new communication behaviours in the organization; to introduce an intranet to enable employees to 'pull' information; and to develop the capability of the internal communication team to deliver this challenging strategy, with all the non-traditional communication skills it demanded. The latter has resulted in such a growth in perceived value that internal communicators are increasingly being asked to join key management initiative discussions to advise on how communication can help.

Evaluation

Throughout the programme, evaluation has been built into the development of the internal communication activities. This has enabled learning from initial effectiveness to steer changes to approach and execution. The previous sections detail how each action has achieved its objectives and is contributing to the overall strategic internal communication objectives. In addition, independent research with the board and key senior managers shows that they now view the internal communication team to be of significant value to the organization.

Indications so far, via focus groups to develop the questionnaire-based research, are that good progress on the objectives has been achieved. In particular, the research will enable an assessment of whether it is just coincidence that the zone that had 50 per cent staff attendance at Railshows, that pushed forward on many of the other actions and in which the IC manager is seen as a commercially focused adviser to the Executive, is also the zone with the best performance. But the internal communication team is not being complacent. It knows there are pockets that have not been sufficiently influenced. The team is working on developing a strategy and action plan through to 2001 and is probing the business (itself fundamentally rethinking strategy) about the imperatives to be supported. It is also strengthening its links with a substantially remodelled and upgraded HR team to ensure consistency of message with people management and development processes.

Gerald Corbett said: 'As chief executive I need people at all levels to understand where we are heading and why. That's vital if they are to be able to make effective contributions to the way we run our business. Our internal communications are now focused on business issues and are developing a valuable dialogue up, down and across the company.'

5

Beyond 'customer is king': public relations strategy in a marketing context

The relationship between marketing and public relations has had a chequered history in the past 10 years. Some would argue that they have been involved in a power struggle for longer than that. In 1978, Kotler and Mindak wrote that there were four levels of public relations activity for marketing purposes, the first being for small, often charitable, organizations who, until recently, rarely outsourced professional public relations or marketing services. A second group, mainly from the public sector, do engage public relations services while a third, small manufacturing companies, often use external marketing services or in-house sales personnel. Fourthly, in large Fortune 500 companies, public relations and marketing are usually separate departments, which may complement each other. In the past, they were coordinated by the chief public relations officer who would report to the CEO and the main board. Today's integrated communication strategies combine the managerial tactics of market research, advertising and public relations theory and practice.

SKILL AND KNOWLEDGE

The traditional qualifying route into public relations was the Communications, Advertising and Marketing Diploma (CAM). However, in the 1990s, a more substantive approach to education and training emerged through the Institute of Public Relations for public relations development, the Institute of Advertising for advertising development and the Chartered Institute of Marketing for marketing development. In blue chip companies, marketing, advertising and public relations functions are linked independently to the corporate and business plans but managed overall as corporate communication. Clearly each function is accountable for its own strategic analysis, segments and targeting of those stakeholders for which they are responsible, but the overall organization's image or reputation must not be compromised by any one function. Of course, all three areas overlap at the boundary between themselves and at the interface between the organization and its environment, with the consequence that environmental monitoring and research are pertinent to each area of activity. It is here that the focus of each function must be independent of the other to maintain plurality of views and richness of information. However, the various perspectives must be brought together at a later stage for integration, then linked strategically with other functions such as HRM since environmental intelligence will have relevance for a range of internal functions.

Strategic planning for all three areas incorporates analysis, monitoring of individual programme development, implementation control and evaluation. If there is a lack of control over any one of the three areas, say one attempting to dominate another for competitive budgeting or status purposes, then the public relations strategy is put at risk. Currently, much rivalry is invoked at both practitioner and academic levels.

CORPORATE INTELLIGENCE

As the amount of information flowing in and out of every organization increases with the Internet and far exceeds any public relations strategist's requirement, the key task of any adequate intelligence system is to access and capture only relevant data and direct it to the required location for analysis by the right group at the right time. A focus on capturing and using pertinent marketing communication data, for example, will not necessarily help service the needs of the advertising or public relations group as it may be too customer specific at the expense of other stakeholders if not moderated by the communication strategist or overseer. Some large firms have comprehensive management information systems and the development of new technologies is increasingly making the selection and identification of critical data easier. Because of the need for longer-term relationships with customers, marketing professionals have been quick to realize the need for systematic design, collection, analysis and reporting of data and findings relevant to the mutual understanding and sustaining of goodwill, traditionally seen as a customer relations/public relations activity, but increasingly coming under the auspices of customer loyalty and referred to by marketers as relationship marketing.

In terms of environmental scanning, market researchers analyse and categorize the environment in a number of ways. A common approach to strategic marketing is one where the philosophy implies that all organizations exist because they are offering some form of 'product' to someone else, whether it be direct, such as biscuits and other fast-moving consumer goods (FMCG), a service offered through a third party and perhaps paid for by a third party (say, government) or a service in the community or to achieve a social objective.

WHAT'S IN A NAME?

Some of the rivalry referred to earlier between marketing and public relations departments in organizations has been around the issue of whether or not the principal stakeholder group or customer 'audience' ought to define the department's name. Traditionally, even though the communication tools and techniques available may be drawn on by all three functions of marketing, advertising and public relations, the dominant strategic force remains with public relations which views its constituencies as consisting of a broader range of stakeholder groups or publics from customers to include competitors and suppliers, but also employers/employees, community and local government, central government, financiers, investors and the media. Only an independent corporate PRO is trained to appraise all ongoing stakeholder relations to ensure that the organization's strategic communication plan is coherent and consistent in relation to the strategic business plan.

VALUE-ADDED PUBLIC RELATIONS

Of particular value to market research professionals has been the public relations evaluation concept of value added, an accounting process which involves horizontal analysis of the industry a firm finds itself in, along with a vertical study of the overall distribution chains to see where value can be improved and competitive advantage gained by strategic repositioning or sales reconfiguration. Another important technique which overlaps with public relations is market segmentation. Guiltinan and Paul (1994) define market segmentation as 'the process of identifying groups of customers with highly similar buying needs and motives within the relevant market'. Segments are formed by identifying response differences between segments. They can be clearly described, reached and are worthwhile as benefits to the organization. They are stable over time so marketing programmes can fix costs to be acceptable. They will be classified using descriptive categories based on management's knowledge and experience of customer need or desires supported by available information (customer group identification), or by the way customers respond. Groups can be identified by working backwards, for example noting characteristics such as the frequency of individual or group purchases or perceptions of brand preference.

Communication theory is grounded in models of perception from clinical psychology, a key factor in public relations academic modelling. Thus, another tool that is increasingly popular is the use of perceptual mapping, where consumer perceptions of product attributes can be analysed psychologically. On the two-dimensional perceptual map, consumers' reception is grouped together with competitive brands to demonstrate position and relationship.

Perhaps the most popular theory of the past 15 years has been Porter's (1985) five competitive forces in determining industry profitability which can clearly be adapted to organizational-level monitoring and evaluation through perceptual mapping and intelligence communication. Perceptual mapping is a technique which identifies gaps in the market to see if there is scope for a new product or to plan branding or competing products in terms of particular characteristics such as price and quality. It is a useful concept for integrating marketing communication with corporate communication to ensure that publicity is coherent and consistent with the aims of corporate communication programmes, or 'on message' as the politicians say. Such analysis can produce public relations intelligence that feeds into the research, monitoring and evaluation information paradigm (Figure 5.1).

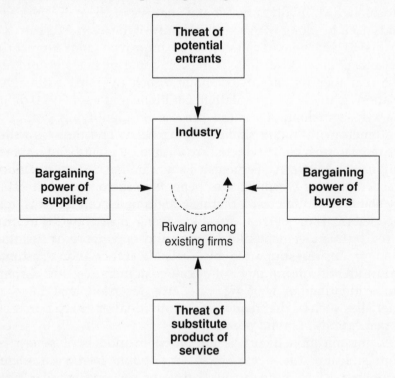

Figure 5.1 *Public relations intelligence*

Source: Porter (1985)

The importance of theoretical models such as Porter's lies in its focus on the competitor stakeholder group and the subgroups within it, such as rivalry between existing competitors, the threat of entry from new niche competitors and the financial muscle of buyers and suppliers. The dynamic nature of competition and thus short- and longer-term relationship building is central to public relations involvement, especially for lobbyists.

Increasingly, interest has been shown by the public relations industry in the notion that marketing public relations techniques can be applied to the competitive internal environment of an organization, because of the political nature of competition for jobs and status.

Where once this was the domain of the PRO, today it is sometimes thought that the marketing director is as likely to be aware of the corporate climate, structure and culture as other experts and that their knowledge and sensitivity to culture, orientation, power and influence will have been accrued from their analysis of customers, organizational structure linked to the marketing plan and the interfunctional dynamics needed to operate that marketing plan.

COMPETITIVE ADVANTAGE

Porter's theories of competitive advantage suggest that it is essential that organizations understand how the physical, human, financial and intangible aspects of an organization, including plant, equipment, people and finance, must be appraised together so as to quantify added value to the customer and thus to the organization as a whole. In addition to showing, through his external analysis, that the organization needs always to consider its role in the overall value chain of suppliers, wholesalers and retailers to the consumer, he originally suggested a generic value chain as shown in Figure 5.2.

It was at this point that the techniques from public relations became so important to marketers. With the growth in service marketing and the development of relationship marketing, more and more organizations were adopting customer awareness programmes to harness the organization's effort to deliver improved value to their customers. This coincided with a general global economic recession which meant that, although traditional

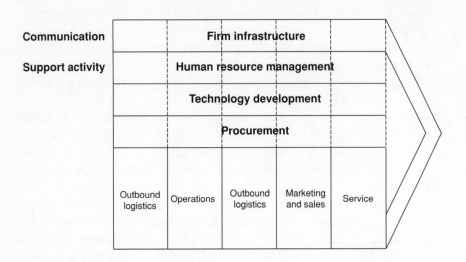

Figure 5.2   *Porter's generic value chain*

Source: Porter (1985)

public relations departments had been removed or downsized, the need for public relations techniques remained. Market research departments found themselves on a fast learning curve in order to adopt the public relations skills and techniques required to cope with their sales and marketing strategies, given the rapid rise of consumer awareness and pressure groups. Customers not only had access to IT and media, but were now well organized and increasingly vociferous in their demands for value for money. If a particular product or brand attracted bad publicity, this could impact on corporate image, identity or reputation to the extent that the overall public relations strategy could be undermined, not least in respect of shareholder investment.

From the point of view of the overall planning process, stake-holder communication must be integrated around core corporate values, objectified by the production of mission statements. Representing the vision of what the organization is or hopes to become, the PRO collates the communication aims and objectives of each function, assesses compatibility and integrates it with the corporate business plan.

Porter's model suggests that there are three fundamental ways in which firms achieve sustainable competitive advantage through customer relations. These are cost leadership strategy, differentiation strategy and focus strategy. The difference between strategic marketing which seeks to interpret the organization's generic strategies into market-based strategies based on perceived added value is that it is dominated by price.

Other writers such as Grunig and Repper (Grunig, 1992, ch 6) believe that the interdependence of stakeholder groups in the achievement of organizational objectives reaffirms the strategic role of public relations in the goals encapsulated by a mission statement.

Most marketing becomes strategic at some point because of the range of options available and so the academic literature concentrates on issues of strategic choice, target market strategy, marketing strategies with demand, positioning strategies and marketing strategies for different environments. The strategy adopted will depend on whether the organization is a market leader with 45 per cent market share, a market challenger with 30 per cent market share, a market follower with 20 per cent market share or a market niche with 10 per cent of the market share (Kotler, 1994). Intelligence data from each market share will drive any public relations imperative.

OVERLAP

Other areas of promotional overlap with public relations are in the marketing of fast-moving consumer goods, as previously mentioned, and business-to-business markets. Consumer markets are characterized by heavy advertising and promotion programmes targeted at key segments so as to build brands and speed up the process of innovation and new product development. They also seek strategic relationships and alternative channels of distribution such as direct marketing and selling via the Internet.

BUSINESS TO BUSINESS

In business-to-business markets or industrial markets, relationship marketing is critical to success, with particular emphasis on conferences and trade shows. Kotler also identified three types of strategic marketing in service industries by naming the company, employees and customers as being linked by internal marketing, external marketing and interactive marketing. With services marketing, the different attributes of the service are identified or organized to target customer value and to position the organization to obtain differential or competitive advantage. A public relations service must be able to articulate and prioritize any or all attributes offered by the service or organization in order to target customer value and to position the organization for competitive customer advantage, as Jobber (1995) shows (Figure 5.3).

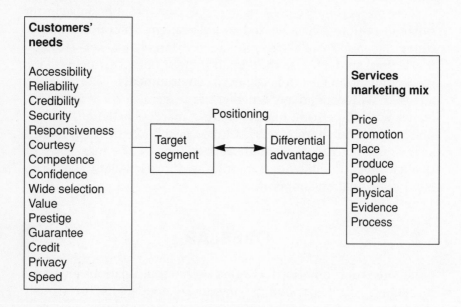

Figure 5.3   *Prioritizing attributes*

Source: Jobber (1995)

As organizations increasingly enter global markets, strategic market decisions are based on international research and may include looking for similarities between segments in different countries with a combination of factor and cluster analysis to identify meaningful cross-national segments.

EVALUATION

This has driven the PR industry to look for new ways of measuring impact of messages across diverse cultures and in shorter time frames. With export marketing, for example, products produced are sold from the domestic base. With international marketing, products and services are marketed across national borders and within foreign countries. With global marketing, coordination of the market strategy in multiple markets operates in the face of global competition. One of the principal strategic concerns in the latter case is the task of developing the global portfolio, which involves a very high level of involvement of both marketing and public relations departments in developing e-commerce and promotional Web pages as part of the strategic public relations plan.

EFFECTIVENESS

Effectiveness of all strategies depends on the quality of the monitoring and environment scanning within different environments, which are in a constant state of change. Of particular concern to the PRO is the problem of control. Not all marketing departments make clear strategy statements which are comprehensive or articulate the interdependence and interaction of the various elements so that the total mix is achieved in a harmonious way. Many a product promotion has created communications and public relations disasters while scandals became focused solely on the customer and omitted to consider the corporate image.

The development of branding theory and practice has reduced some of this difficulty, but at the same time has created semantic confusion when describing activities relating to both marketing and public relations. For example, Cravens (1994) says that 'a product is anything that is potentially valued by a target market for the benefits or satisfactions it provides, including objects, services, organization, places, people and ideas'. This description covers both tangible and intangible services and could conceivably include all the other stakeholders, outside consumers and customers.

Brand promotion, including corporate advertising, is a traditional public relations tool for adding value to a product so as to differentiate it from its competitors or to add value to the corporate identity. However, not all marketers see it this way, nor indeed do all other professional departments in the organization. Finance, for example, may be involved in designing pricing strategy, given, as Kotler says, that 'price is the only element in the marketing mix that produces revenue. The other elements produce costs.'

TOOLS AND TECHNIQUES

The role of advertising and publicity is to be cost effective in creating awareness in the early stages of the product life cycle whereas sales promotion is used in the ordering and reordering stages of buyer readiness where the product is mature or in decline. Kotler's view of the tools and characteristics of communication are seen as shown in Table 5.1.

Table 5.1 *Kotler's view of tools and characteristics*

Tools	Characteristics
Advertising	Public presentation, pervasive, amplified expressiveness. TV, radio, press, cinema, magazines, print, packaging, posters
Product/service promotion	Gain attention, provide information, inducement that gives value, invitation to engage in immediate action; competitions, premiums, gifts, trade shows, coupons, stamps
Direct marketing publicity	Direct at consumer, customized, up to date; catalogues, mailings, telemarkets, electronic shopping
Public relations	High credibility, messages as news not advertising; press kits, seminars, annual reports, sponsorships, lobbying
Customer relations (sales)	Personal confrontation, cultivates relationships, encourages response; presentations, incentives, samples, trade shows

Source: Adapted from Kotler (1994)

Christopher *et al* (1994) suggest that 'relationship marketing has as its concern the dual focus of getting and keeping customers'. Indeed, they go on to develop a model which suggests that there are five other markets that impact on the customer market, namely referral markets, internal markets, supplier markets, employee recruitment markets and influence markets, and if marketing people are to tinker with all these particular audiences, the role of the PRO becomes imperative. It is apparent that they are working towards the stakeholder model and at some point will realize that they are in the business of public relations and not just customer relations (Table 5.2).

Table 5.2 *Towards integration*

Bottom-line approach	**Value added approach**
Transaction marketing	**Relationship marketing**
Focus on single sale	Focus on customer retention
Orientation on product features	Orientation on product benefits
Short time-scale	Long time-scale
Little emphasis on customer service	High customer service emphasis
Limited customer commitment	High customer commitment
Moderate customer contact	High customer contact
Quality concern of production	Quality concern of all

Source: Christopher *et al* (1994)

As with any policy-making, planning and strategic development, evaluation and control is of paramount importance. A strategic review of marketing plans is usually conducted every two or three years to provide groundwork for long-term strategy development as well as interim analysis. It will usually consist of a full marketing audit of the marketing environment and operations relating to all aspects of the corporate mission, objectives and strategies, as well as a review of the marketing objectives, strategies, programmes, implementation and management issues.

PERFORMANCE CRITERIA

As with public relations and advertising campaigns, reviews are essential in examining the extent to which programmes are appropriately directed and whether or not a particular programme has been effective for the organization as a whole. This may include an excellence review where benchmarking takes place against external examples of best practice, which also involve ethical and social responsibility criteria. Some of the performance criteria and measures used by marketing functions are sales analysis, market share analysis, sales to expense ratios, financial analysis and profitability analysis. This is a costly process and the results will be compared with various internal budgets, targets and performance measures set by the corporation.

PERFORMANCE GAPS

It is at this point that any positive or negative performance gaps, new opportunities or threats may require corrective action to bring the annual plan or longer-term strategy back in line with objectives. The requirement is often to identify the difference between problems, symptoms and causes that cannot be ignored from seasonal or short-term variations. Third party intervention from public relations consultants is often bought in, in conjunction with other management consultants. Where, for instance, some inter-functional relationship problems experienced by marketing and manufacturing departments cannot be managed effectively, consultants can provide an objective solution. Typically, problems that emerge are that products are developed around technological capability, not market needs; products may fail commercially; products may be technically superior but priced too high; and concentration on tangible attributes may supersede the customer benefits. Indeed, some organizations have placed research and development and marketing under one authority, in physical close proximity, or set up coordination teams or task groups on particular projects. The role of public relations may be to advise on internal or external communication processes, including impacts on corporate identity.

MARKETING VS MANUFACTURING

Other areas of inter-functional conflict may be: marketing who want more capacity versus manufacturing who want accurate sales forecasts; marketing who want faster response versus manufacturing who want consistent production; marketing who want sufficient stocks versus manufacturing who want cost control; marketing who want quality assurance whereas manufacturing have products which are difficult to make; marketing who want variety whereas manufacturing want economical runs; marketing who want low prices and high service whereas manufacturing often have high costs with extra services; and marketing always looking for new products whereas manufacturing see extra design and tooling costs. Competent communication skills between departmental heads are crucial, although few will realize that they are involved in public relations.

So what we have seen at a strategic level is the need for integration of all elements of the communication mix, while, at a tactical level, some of the tools employed when implementing and evaluating programmes can be shared.

As Smith and O'Neill (1997) said: 'Marketing used to be simple. So simple, it could even be left to marketing managers, but it isn't like that any more. The business of marketing – namely creating value by managing customer relationships – must be central to corporate management and financial planning. Marketing must be seamlessly woven into every function of those companies intent on getting to the future first.' The following case study demonstrates this view.

SUMMARY

The application of public relations techniques to marketing objectives was considered in terms of environmental group receptivity, perceptual mapping and competitive advantage. Fundamental strategic public relations approaches to generic concepts were described, including measurable bottom-line factors. Semantic confusion, where it exists, was explained particularly in relation to branding. Integrated communicated strategies call for corporate control where all activities, including product and service advertising, operate within the framework of the corporate public relations strategy to ensure coherence and consistency.

CASE STUDY: THE BODY SHOP CANADA

Published by kind permission of IPRA.

Introduction

In 1998, The Body Shop Canada (TBSC) wanted to launch a controversial product line which used hemp seed oil in its ingredients. The government wanted it banned and the marketing launch threatened to become a major crisis for the image and reputation of the company. An open and ethical strategic PR approach to all its marketing communication led to measurable value-added corporate branding as well as successful introduction of a new product range.

The case illustrates the need to prepare alternative campaigns around a coherent corporate message.

- It had well-orchestrated coverage with one stakeholder group (media) while maintaining a non-confrontational stance with another (the regulatory body).
- It had a high-profile campaign to use the acceptable face of its CEO.

THE BODY SHOP CANADA

The problem

In October 1998, The Body Shop Canada (TBSC) launched its innovative Hemp range – a controversial product line featuring hemp seed oil. A consultancy firm, Strategic Objectives (SOI), was responsible for researching and developing the marketing launch programme. Just 72 hours before the launch event, Health Canada – Canada's Federal Government regulatory body – informed them that the hemp products might be seized if they proceeded with the launch. They immediately restructured the national marketing programme and proceeded with a revised 'Maybe Yes, Maybe No Hemp Product Launch'. Media and customer response across Canada was overwhelming. Sales beat all forecasts.

TBSC, with more than 121 shops across Canada, does not advertise. TBSC depends on word of mouth from its customers and the media to build its brand; to fuel positive awareness and demand for its excellent, innovative products; and to support its bold stands on issues of public concern.

Research

In March 1998, TBSC confirmed it would start the process to bring the company's Hemp Dry Skin Treatment range – an innovative, first-of-its-kind product range featuring the moisturizing properties of industrial hemp seed oil – to Canada. For the next eight months, The Body Shop worked with the Canadian Government to meet all regulations on hemp products. TBSC Hemp products finally passed all required tests and the product was shipped with full documentation *legally* into Canada in early September.

Because this was a controversial product, the consultants analysed The Body Shop's previous launch activities and media/consumer response to hemp in the UK, Italy and the United States. They wanted to ensure that the Canadian marketing programme aligned with the global launch plan.

In Canada, hemp was making news as a new crop and a new hope for Canadian farmers. The consultancy researched hemp farming in Canada – networking with national experts, including The Body Shop's Canadian supplier of hemp seed oil – and identified key hemp advocates in the federal government. They determined the credible influencers on this issue and enlisted their participation in The Body Shop Hemp launch, to add to the credibility and efficacy of hemp.

Planning

With only five weeks to the retail launch of hemp, TBSC authorized the consultancy to develop a PR marketing communication programme as advertising would not be utilized. A media launch event date of Monday, 5 October 1998 was set. Anita Roddick, founder of The Body

Shop International, agreed to participate in the marketing activities. They determined that the launch must:

- introduce, explain, and gain credibility for TBS Hemp as a safe, effective and desirable treatment for dry skin;
- make positive news that would drive sales and customer traffic;
- manage issues and misinformation around hemp and clearly distinguish it from its controversial cousin, marijuana.

The strategy transformed unexpectedly into a crisis issues management programme when Health Canada announced that it would seize the hemp product if TBSC introduced it at the event or in shops. This news came just 72 hours before the scheduled launch. With the safety of a TBSC product line in question, there was an urgent need for marketing communications to protect the reputation and good name of The Body Shop and the credibility of hemp. Faced with these new issues, the launch had to:

- meet a challenge to TBSC's good name with smart ideas and better solutions;
- turn adversity into triumph by fusing creativity with proactivity;
- prove that good marketing sells.

COMMUNICATION

They produced a media kit which:

- was fun and informative and included information on the unique hemp range from TBSC. It also spotlighted the history of hemp through the ages.
- created an editorial product photograph that incorporated actual hemp leaves. Because the Government of Canada regulations do not allow hemp leaves to leave a hemp farm, the photograph was shot on-site at a hemp farm.
- developed good answers to tough questions to help TBSC spokespeople and shop staff deal with media and consumer confusion around hemp and marijuana.

Target audience

The ultimate goal was to reach TBSC target customers – well-educated, adult Canadians – to educate them on the Hemp range and encourage them to try it and buy it at their nearest location of The Body Shop. To reach these consumers, the consultants communicated with key media contacts from Canada's local, regional and national news; fashion; health and wellness; business; lifestyle; retail; as well as reporters covering the hemp issue in Canada and nutriceuticals and trends journalists.

Creative event planned

They invited the media to preview and celebrate the arrival of hemp, at a media launch on Monday, 5 October 1998. Hemp was scheduled to be launched in all 121 locations of The Body Shop across Canada on the following Thursday, 8 October 1998. The event concept and public awareness programme were developed to reflect the irreverent, bold spirit of TBSC and spotlight hemp and its versatility:

- Anita Roddick gave a day of media interviews, beginning at 6:40 am with the last interview scheduled to air just after midnight.
- A fun Hemp Media Event press pack was faxed to key Toronto-based media contacts, two weeks prior to the event, and it was distributed again via Canada Newswire on the Friday prior to the Monday launch.
- A more formal printed invitation was distributed to media and key hemp advocates, along with a package of hemp seed snacks.
- The event was planned for the Gypsy Co-op in Toronto, a counter-culture restaurant.
- A pro-hemp panel of speakers was organized, including: Anita Roddick; Margot Franssen, President and Partner, TBSC; Senator Lorna Milne, a Canadian senator, active in the legalization of hemp in Canada; Kelley Fitzpatrick, a nutriceuticals expert in the benefits of hemp seed oil in cosmetics; and Ruth Shamai, a Canadian hemp farmer, and hemp seed oil supplier to TBS.
- To demonstrate the versatility of the hemp plant, the consultancy sourced and imported legal hemp wine, hemp beer, hemp pretzels, hemp fabric, hemp clothing, and hemp-based food for the event.
- Signage focused on the hemp product range and the hemp leaf icon.

IMPLEMENTATION

On Friday, 2 October 1998 at 11:30 am, the consultancy received a call from Health Canada, advising them and TBSC that they might have to cancel the Monday launch. They were told that if the hemp launch went ahead, TBSC hemp products could be seized because Health Canada was concerned about multiple exposure of hemp. Both TBSC and the consultancy could be in contravention of the law that might be enacted. This demanded a new plan:

- A cross-functional crisis/communications team was struck – TBSC, its lawyers and consultants weighed the pros and cons of moving ahead with the launch.
- They worked with Health Canada to seek a resolution throughout the weekend and kept TBSC franchisees and staff in the loop.
- They requested an emergency meeting with Health Canada for Monday morning (the scheduled day of the launch) and flew in Dr David Hitchen, The Body Shop International's hemp expert, to share his knowledge with Health Canada officials.
- They recommended that TBSC be true to The Body Shop brand – open and honest – and go forward with a non-product hemp launch. The consultants named it the 'Maybe Yes, Maybe No Hemp Product Launch'.
- They apprised event speakers of the situation so that they could re-evaluate their participation and alter their speeches accordingly. This communication was ongoing throughout the weekend.

Over the weekend, they changed almost every aspect of the 'Maybe Yes, Maybe No Hemp Launch':

- All new media materials were created.
- Two sets of speeches were prepared – one geared to Health Canada giving The Body Shop Canada the 'okay' to launch the product and one announcing that it could not be launched.
- Because Health Canada was concerned about 'multiple exposures' to hemp products, the hemp food, wine and beer were cancelled. Catering was replaced with more traditional fare.
- In order to comply with potential Health Canada concerns, blackout bars were placed over the product names on signage.
- No one was allowed to 'sample' the range, so the consultancy actually glued the hemp product to the displays so that no one could try it or take it away.
- A special publication, 'Hemp Full Voice', was printed for the event. To comply with Health Canada concerns, the pages featuring the product were glued together.
- TBSC speakers and senior management, including Anita Roddick, were debriefed the night before the event.

The day of the launch

- An emergency meeting was held at the consultancy with invited hemp activists to answer their immediate questions.

- A new press release was distributed at 6 am to let the media know that the story had changed and Anita broke the story on national TV, CBC Newsworld, live at 6:40 am.
- The event was packed with TV cameras and reporters from top magazines, newspapers and radio.
- The hemp product launch was successfully repositioned as hard news.
- TBSC told the hemp story, and a panel provided third-party endorsement.
- An emergency meeting was held in Ottawa so that Health Canada could hear from BSI head chemist and TBSC partner, Quig Tingley.
- A revised news release was sent out on the newswire to time with the noon media launch event.

Event results

- TBSC's Hemp story made news across Canada throughout the day, and for weeks to come, with a constant layering of The Body Shop Hemp messages.
- Key marketing messages about hemp reached Canadians via the media from the time they woke up, throughout the day, and right up to Mike Bullard – a comedy TV interview programme – in the late evening.
- Health Canada was inundated with media inquiries and requests for a statement.
- The emergency meeting between Health Canada and TBSC was productive, and by 6 pm, the matter was resolved – The Body Shop Canada was permitted to sell its Hemp Dry Skin Treatment range without risk of seizure from Health Canada.
- The good news was issued in an update news release and distributed on the newswire.
- A complete media kit was distributed to key health and beauty journalists, along with a hemp product sample, since it had now become legal.

Grassroots Advertising, a postering company booked to plaster TBSC hemp posters on hoardings in the cities of Toronto, Montreal and Vancouver and then cancelled, was re-booked, once the product was approved.

The challenge

Health Canada's last-minute decision to 'potentially ban' the sale of the TBSC Hemp range meant that TBSC/SOI had to go into crisis mode, working non-stop throughout the weekend to revise the event and the messages. Three hundred and twenty man-hours were condensed into

101

a single weekend, demanding that the team operate on very little sleep. Ensuring that TBSC stayed within the law on this issue was of utmost importance, as was working with Health Canada to find a resolution. The decision not to back down nor to cancel the event was bold, but true to the TBSC cultural style. The challenge was not to minimize the seriousness of the 'ban' nor to jeopardize TBSC's relationship with Health Canada officials, but still to stage a memorable, fun and irreverent marketing launch. The events demonstrated TBSC transparency and successfully explained the hemp story. In doing so, it garnered wide media interest and coverage that conveyed their key messages.

Evaluation

All marketing messages for the launch of hemp were successfully communicated. The Body Shop 'Maybe Yes, Maybe No Hemp Product Launch' was one of the most successful launches in TBSC's 20-year history. The marketing programme attracted new customers to TBSC, with shop staff reporting that nearly every customer had heard of the TBSC Hemp range and had come in to 'check it out'. Sales beat TBSC's optimistic forecasts and many of the products sold out across Canada within the first month. The product range enhanced TBSC brand equity and TBSC was portrayed as an innovative trailblazer in the cosmetics industry and a powerful voice for the credibility of hemp.

It was virtually impossible to miss the media coverage, whether on the radio, television or in the newspapers from coast to coast. In the first week alone, there were 183 print and electronic media stories and audience reach exceeded 11.9 million Canadians. All coverage positively conveyed the TBSC position. Coverage in all key beauty magazines was generated, leading to exceptional consumer demand. Advertising equivalency audit value (PR factor of three) was $1.3 million.

The credibility and success of both TBSC and their agency were greatly enhanced. TBSC had an excellent year and the agency attracted new public relations clients. Relations with Health Canada continued to be strong and progressive.

6

Time, talent and creativity: public relations strategy in a multimedia context

Mass communication media has come to play a dominant role in the life of everyone, including the public relations practitioner. With the growth and convergence of global telecommunications and information technology, the role of these media can only become even more important in the future, the Internet being just one example. Few people, let alone organizations of all kinds, dare to forecast where this will lead in the future other than to suggest that the media will play a vital role in the survival of every organization.

Most large organizations employ agencies to monitor the media and to communicate with journalists, proprietors and other significant persons in institutions who could be instrumental in the maintenance of an organization's corporate aims and objectives.

Strategically, this role can be seen as a defensive, asymmetrical relationship or, in more enlightened far-seeing organizations, as a creative, symmetrical relationship, through which the organization can obtain the information necessary to be able to adapt to a changing environment.

MASS COMMUNICATION

The significance of the media of mass communication on an organization cannot be overestimated. McQuail (1994) ascribes five characteristics to the media which explain their importance to society as a whole. These are relevant to the modern organization at all stages of a public relations campaign or programme. The five characteristics are:

1. *A power resource*. This is highly relevant to organizations, given that the media are the primary means of transmission and source of information in society. A disgruntled shareholder wishing to unseat a member of the board will find it difficult to communicate with other shareholders in the face of the power that the organization's managers can rally.
2. *The arena of public affairs*. For business organizations, this may seem less important than for governmental organizations which are often the target of media attention, but many recent inter-company controversies involving government agencies have been played out in the arena of the media.
3. *Definitions of social reality*. At first sight, this is a nebulous concept and yet McQuail explains that the media is a place where the changing culture and the values of society and groups are constructed, stored and visibly expressed. What society perceives to be the reality of organizations will be formed from a limited or non-existent personal impression gained from direct contact with the organization and from those images and impressions which the media choose to present. Different sections of the media attempt to project different realities. For example, in the UK, the BBC *Money Programme* presents a world in which it is normal for companies to compete with each other for profit without implying any criticism of the underlying capitalist principles involved. Left-wing publications will, on the other hand, portray a

different version of reality, one that is much more critical and sceptical about the motives and social value of the leaders of major firms.

4. *The primary key to fame and celebrity status*. This used not to be particularly important as far as business organizations were concerned. However, increasingly, leaders of organizations have used the media in order to project a desirable image. This is also true for authors of texts of strategic management theory who have become highly rewarded 'gurus' on the international lecture circuit.

5. *As a benchmark for what is normal*. This is particularly important for organizations when ethical issues are concerned. Currently, business organizations are having to face up to the new norms of environmental concerns, corporate social responsibility and other matters. Economic criteria used to take precedence over the views of fringe environmental groups, but the media now define normality as one in which an endangered environment must be protected and form part of the criteria for competent management. In the early 1990s, Shell came unstuck over the proposed deep-sea disposal of the Brent Spar oil rig, despite their eminently rational cost–benefit analysis which attempted to bring environmental issues into the equation. To cope with this, McQuail presents a two-dimensional framework for representing contrasting theoretical perspectives (see Figure 6.1).

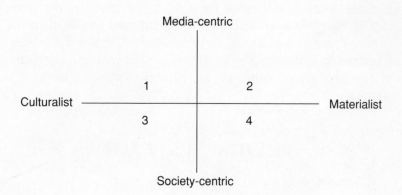

Figure 6.1 *Perspectives on media and society*

Source: McQuail (1994)

MEDIA-CENTRIC/SOCIETY-CENTRIC

The media-centric/society-centric dimension contrasts approaches which focus on the media's own sphere of activity and see it as a primary mover in social change, as opposed to where the media are seen as reflecting wider political, social and economic forces. The other dimension takes a view which emphasizes culture and ideas as opposed to material forces and factors. McQuail sees these two dimensions as being independent. This allows four different perspectives on media and society, as shown in Figure 6.1.

MEDIA CULTURIST/MEDIA MATERIALIST

The corporate communication or business strategy of a firm at any particular moment or situation will influence the approach taken by the public relations planner. From a media/culturalist view, an organization might concentrate on the content and reception of media messages; for example, whether a public relations campaign to convince the public that the organization improved the environment was being received by active members of the green movement in the way the organization desired. A media/materialist approach, for example, would look at the role that technological developments such as the Internet were having on the media channels available to the public relations programme. A social/culturalist approach offers less of an emphasis on the media itself than on its social role, particularly the role of the press in influencing social and political attitudes. Finally, a social/materialist perspective would see the media and its influence as deriving from economic and material conditions in society, and this would be an extreme example of McQuail's quadrant.

RHETORIC VS REALITY

Large organizations rely on mass communication, particularly in the form of advertising. In addition to informing the public about products and services and inducing them to buy, they communicate messages about the nature of the organization and its values, which may or may not reflect objective reality. Nicholas Ind (1997) believes that public relations activity fulfils a not dissimilar strategic role to advertising 'in that its function is to increase awareness and improve favourability, but loses out to advertising in its controllability'. He uses as an example the American Anti-slavery Society, one of the longest and oldest public relations strategies, which was formed in 1833 and established its own newspapers, held public meetings, distributed pamphlets and lobbied state legislatures and the US Congress demanding action to abolish slavery. 'Even after the American Civil War, the society still campaigned for constitutional amendments and civil rights laws to protect the gains of the newly freed slave. This led to the passing of the 13th Amendment abolishing slavery.'

The word 'mass' therefore can be given positive, negative or undifferentiated associations depending on the political perspective adopted. For example, positive in socialist rhetoric sees the masses as a source of strength, while negative, when associated with the dictators of the 1930s, subscribes to individualistic and elitist cultural values. However, in a communication context it refers to a large, seemingly undifferentiated audience. This is essentially an asymmetrical stance, because message receivers had little chance to share their perceptions with the mass of other message receivers up until the new technology allowed, for example, chat rooms on the World Wide Web.

COMMUNICATING WITH THE MEDIA

A pluralistic, processual approach to any strategic public relations endeavour inevitably involves the mass media at some point. There are a number of different models which help to show how it might inform the PR manager of an organization today:

1. *The transmission model*. This model views communication as transmitting a fixed amount of information. The sequence of sender—message—channel—receiver is now seen as naive and is replaced by the sequence of events and voices in society, channel/communicator role, message, receiver, thereby recognizing that the mass media are not the originators of the message, but rather that they are relaying their account of a selection of events.

2. *A ritual or expressive model*. The former model implies that there is an instrumental motive in the communication process, that the message is trying to achieve something. However, communication is sometimes seen as a form of ritual when it expresses sharing, participation, association, fellowship and the possession of a common faith. Many advertising campaigns exploit the mass media in this way, not transmitting information about the product or service but rather associating it with a supposedly shared value. For example, a butter product might be associated with factory-produced beer as representing traditional images of rural life and the country inn.

3. *A publicity model*. This sees the sender as not attempting to transmit anything, but rather simply seeking to catch visual or oral attention. The public may see the media not so much as a source of information but as escapism from everyday reality. Many organizations find it possible to exploit this aspect of the mass media, especially organizations such as Greenpeace, who can provide exciting and attention-grabbing film footage such as a motor boat cutting across the bows of a Japanese trawler, which guarantees media attention.

4. *A reception model*. This argues that any meaningful message is built up with signs whose meanings depend on choices made by the sender or encoder. Receivers or decoders are not of course obliged to accept the messages sent. They can put their own interpretation on what they receive and therefore a reception model is dependent on an encoding and decoding process by those involved in sending or receiving communication.

All organizations plan their relationship with the media as part of their overall public relations policy. Here it is not possible to proceed without some comment about the term 'public relations' and the dilemma that the Institute of Public Relations finds itself in in terms of its own identity and reputation. Public relations has acquired a pejorative association in the minds of many people because it has been perceived as being a process by which organizations attempt to conceal the truth about their activities behind a smoke screen. In political circles, a public relations practitioner has become a 'spin doctor' whose narrowly defined function is to deflect public criticism and to defend his or her masters or mistresses from public criticism. The shortened marketing acronym of PR for public relations is symbolic of this and, some argue, has added to the profession's status difficulties as it is often not regarded as a discipline based on reliable and valid empirical methodologies. Educators, therefore, usually avoid its use wherever possible, in the same way as they would not refer to CA for chartered accountancy.

NEW TECHNOLOGIES

Some of the key issues affecting corporate strategy are issues relating to globalization and the new technology, which have brought about the globalization of markets, the development of worldwide networks, a widening of membership for pressure groups and a broader analysis of competition. It therefore seems an almost pointless exercise to plan strategically in a chaotic environment in which the notion of managing risk appears by definition to be a misnomer. If the power of individual nation states to control national economies has become limited, the problems of a borderless world become more acute.

As most public relations practitioners know, campaigns have to be planned at the global level, but acted out at the local level. The importance of region states or areas is defined by some degree of economic logic which may lie within a nation state or cross nation state boundaries. So, just as the relevance of the nation state is being called into question, it is apparent that the modern multinational is continuing to lose what was left of its national character. Reich (1990) gives the example of Whirlpool which now employs 43,500 people around the world in 45 countries, most of them non-Americans. He points out that Texas Instruments does most of its research and development, design and manufacturing in East Asia. Reich believes that a company's most important competitive asset is the skills and cumulative learning of its workforce if it is equipped to compete in the global economy.

Jolly (1996) believes that, to qualify as pursuing a global public relations strategy, a company must be able to demonstrate selective contestability and global resources. Selective contestability is where the corporation can contest any market it chooses to compete in, but can be selective about where it wishes to compete. It is prepared to contest any market should the opportunity arise and is constantly on the global lookout for such. In the marketing communication chapter, we saw that such organizations represent potential new entrants in all global markets.

THINK GLOBAL, ACT LOCAL

The corporation may have to bring its entire worldwide resources to bear on any competitive situation it finds itself in anywhere in the world. Customers know that they are dealing with a global player even if it is employing a local competitive formula. Thus global strategies are not standard product market strategies which assume that the world is a homogenous border-free marketplace. Nor are they just about global presence. If what the corporation does in one country has no relation to what it does in other countries, that is no different from dealing with various domestic competitors. Finally, globalization is not just about large companies; the Internet makes it possible for small companies to trade worldwide.

THE FUTURE

The full potential impact of the Internet cannot yet be assessed, but there is clearly strategic potential for using the Internet as an information channel, for distributing news, for building a communication channel and using it as a transaction channel. Web pages need to be constantly updated and this requires investment in multimedia expertise. The design and research aspects of managing an organization's World Wide Web site are offering growth potential for many public relations agencies and consultancies, albeit their use is very complex in terms of corporate communication planning. The cliché 'think global (big), act local (small)' is no longer enough unless PR evaluation stands up to the rigour of quantitative and qualitative audits.

E-COMMERCE AND PUBLIC RELATIONS THEORY

The impact of e-commerce or corporate communication has led to a debate about whether public relations has become a marketing tool and is no longer appropriate, especially for organizational strategic public relations. Many companies have changed their departmental names to corporate communication instead of public relations to reflect this development.

With the future unknown, the debate centres on the dominant theoretical models as identified by the author (Table 6.1).

Table 6.1 *Dominant theoretical models*

Selected characteristics	Dominant theoretical models		
	Classical PR	Professional PR	Corporate communications
Boundaries	Locus of control	Divergent	Convergent
Orientation	Greeks, Romans Pre-war USA	Post-war US/UK/Europe	Global
Ideology	Paternalistic	Collectivistic	Individualistic
Role	Public control	Systems management	Stakeholder relations
Relationship with main board	Administrative	Advisory/ executive	Strategic
Generic activity	Public affairs	Public relations	Divergent comm.
Status of workforce	Staff	Employees	Professional class
Relations with media	Social	Legal	Psychological
Role of institutes/ unions	Marginal	Adversarial	Collaborative
Change	Slow	Moderate	Continuous
Market position	Protected	Stable	Competitive
Attitude	Social stability	Essential cost	Mutual dependence

CLASSIFICATION OF THE CORPORATE COMMUNICATION CONSULTANT ACTIVITIES

The functions shown in Figure 6.2 make up the professional practice based on typical client consultancy business.

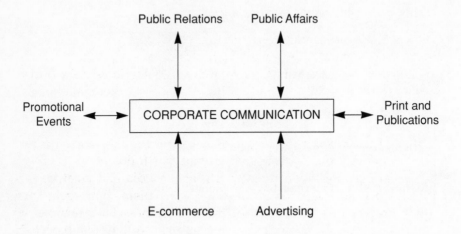

Figure 6.2 *Activities in professional practice*

THE CORPORATE COMMUNICATION ACADEMIC MODEL

The study of corporate communication is based on some or all of the following disciplines, making corporate communication perhaps one of the broadest multi-disciplinary and inter-disciplinary subjects available in universities today. Topics will be studied from:

Politics
Economics
Philosophy
Language, Semiology and Semantics
Cultural Studies

Psychology
Sociology
Computer Studies
Research Methods
Information Studies incl. Library/Archival Sourcing
Journalism incl. writing
Media Studies incl. Mass Communication
Advertising
Marketing
Business Studies incl. transaction theory
Management Studies incl. change strategies
Human Resource Management incl. Organizational Behaviour
Law
Ethics

Universities make choices between including the study of this discipline in Media Arts departmental portfolios or in Business and Management department portfolios. Media and creative arts faculty people approach PR through journalism, film, radio and photography production (for events/publicity etc) while business faculty approach PR through a management orientation based on planning and control. Hands-on skills are learnt through workshops sometimes provided by trainers/visitors, just as they are in courses on accountancy, marketing and IT.

E-COMMERCE

Communication students should understand the fundamental concepts of e-commerce technical infrastructure and applications. This includes electronic commerce and law; security and authentication; and Internet protocols for knowledge-economy companies. These are key competencies for consultant practitioners who are expected to offer strategic corporate e-learning communication solutions for business and commerce (see Table 6.1, Relationship with main board). Furthermore, an understanding of the value/supply chain, with all its communication interfaces and the implications of an e-enabled supply chain, is essential.

CONVERGENT COMMUNICATION

Convergence of traditional telecommunications industries came about because the 'time-to-market' for communications technologies narrowed from 20 years to 6 months during the 1990s. This convergence has led to some of the most lucrative consultancy in the corporate communication profession as industry tries to cope with the rapid rate of change in company and commercial cultures. Thus we see that corporate communication is both divergent and convergent in theory and practice, requiring special, advanced multi-skilling and powers of strategic thinking and operational practice.

PUBLIC RELATIONS

The IPR definition of the term public relations as being 'about reputation – the result of what you do, what you say and what other say about you' can be understood conceptually at numerous levels.

The IPR definition of public relations practice is 'the discipline which looks after reputation – with the aim of earning understanding and support, and influencing opinion and behaviour. It is the planned and sustained effort to establish and maintain goodwill and mutual understanding between an organization and its publics.' This becomes increasingly complex in the light of the new technologies. Therefore, many IPR members reject the notion of a change of terminology and argue that the above definitions incorporate the impact of electronics as simply new operational tools which don't impact on meaning. However, given that technology has so changed the operational management of all forms of business and organizational communication and given that communication is the key measurable variable in the subject, the term corporate communication better represents theory and practice of this discipline for large organizations.

SUMMARY

PR strategies must take into account the characteristics of today's media and the importance of the Internet. A framework for contrasting theories was considered and the difference between public relations message communication and propaganda was noted with a reference to the transfer process model.

CASE STUDY: THE GESTETNER COMPANY, BRITAIN

Published by kind permission of IPRA.

Introduction

This case demonstrates how a PR campaign based on multimedia exposure on the Internet and television helped to change the image and mission of a firm by taking into account five characteristics of competent strategic planning, namely power, politics, social reality, status and ethical concerns.

Key points

- It recreated image and identity while restoring its stable, traditional reputation for reliability.
- It met short-term marketing objectives and longer-term strategic aims to regain competitive advantage in the IT field.
- It used a variety of creative techniques through diverse audiences from a range of stakeholders, including media, customers, employees.

THE GESTETNER COMPANY

The problem

- Gestetner is a major pan-European digital office equipment company. Research showed that in an age of highly competitive, hi-tech digital technology, Gestetner was perceived as old-fashioned and out of date. The reality is quite the opposite and the company is, in fact, a leading provider of cutting-edge, innovative digital hardware. The problem was to communicate this on a nation-wide scale and to reach IT managers – a different audience from Gestetner's traditional customer base of office equipment managers.

- During 1998–99, Gestetner had a window of opportunity as its new product range leapt ahead of the competition in the world of digital technology.

Research

- The consultancy sought to devise an initiative that positioned Gestetner as innovative, cutting-edge, and ahead of its competitors with a focus on its digital technology. 'Digital' was identified as a key word.
- It was agreed to take a more creative approach and link with an art initiative that demonstrated Gestetner's focus on leading-edge digital technology.
- The consultancy researched the UK's leading digital art experts, leading to liaison with the Royal College of Art, the London Science Museum, the Institute of Contemporary Arts and Middlesex University, using the media and the Internet as a guide.

Recommendation

The Communication Group proposed the sponsorship of an art-technology challenge to the students at the Royal College of Art, to be launched with a ground-breaking work of digital art as their inspiration. The objective was to identify Gestetner with cutting-edge digital technology. The launch of the challenge was to be held at the London Science Museum and then followed by the student exhibition at the Royal College of Art. The Gestetner Digital Art Experience was born.

Planning

Objective

- To position Gestetner at the cutting edge of digital technology.
- To communicate this to Gestetner's commercial targets, and track the company's access to key decision makers, particularly IT managers.

Target audiences

The initiative aimed to stimulate business opportunities for Gestetner through repeated contact with the company's key commercial targets. Therefore, the following audiences were identified:

- IT managers (commercial sector): to establish Gestetner's digital credentials with a new key audience now responsible for office technology, as systems converge.

- Procurement specialists (major accounts and public sector): to cement the relationship with Gestetner's five existing key account customers and generate new business.

The consultancy and Gestetner identified a customer universe of 10,000 contacts to be targeted by the initiative.

Vehicles for communication and management support

- The communication channels operated through a two-phase programme, comprising the launch of a challenge to students at the Royal College of Art to create works of art using digital technology, and an exhibition of the winning entries at the College. The consultancy presented this proposal to the Gestetner management team and their field sales team, who viewed this as an excellent opportunity to access clients and potential clients in an imaginative and unusual way – stimulation and motivation of Gestetner's own sales and marketing team was seen as an important part of the plan.
- A timetable for an initial event to launch the challenge, the development of design prototypes by the students, and an ultimate exhibition of the winning works of digital art, was devised.

Implementation

Plan implementation

Sponsorship of a digital art challenge to the students of the Computer-Related Design department at the Royal College of Art was negotiated, and a work of digital art, by leading digital artist Julie Freeman, was commissioned to act as an inspiration to the students and launch the initiative.

Phase One

- The digital artist, Julie Freeman, was briefed to create a ground-breaking work of digital art, which would be fully interactive, visually spectacular and incorporate Gestetner's digital technology.
- The result was the Gestetner Digital Wave – a 50-foot, fully interactive work of digital art which used state-of-the art digital technology to capture the physical image of a person and send it on a journey of visual transformation along the wave-shaped structure, to be reproduced on Gestetner colour printer copiers, and then onto shirts, as a reminder of their digital journey.
- Supporting press materials, including photography, to publicize the unveiling of the Gestetner Digital Wave were developed and tailored to appeal to a variety of media, from arts and IT correspondents, to the office equipment trade press, to national newspapers and television.

- Over 10,000 of Gestetner's commercial targets were invited to a launch event at the London Science Museum, to unveil the Gestetner Digital Wave and launch the challenge to the students at the Royal College of Art. Guests' children were included as added incentive to attend, making the event atmosphere relaxed and festive as well as commercial and educational.
- Professor Christopher Frayling, Rector of the Royal College of Art, addressed the guests from a dramatic overhead steel bridge in the Science Museum.
- The consultancy negotiated for the Gestetner Digital Wave to be exhibited for a further period at the Institute of Contemporary Arts. It was also exhibited at UMIST as part of the Gestetner Digital Office exhibition, a showcase of office environments.

Phase Two

- The Royal College of Art students were briefed to create their own works of digital art – with a project theme of 'information flow and management'.
- Ten works of digital art were developed to prototype, with five winning entries selected for exhibition at the Royal College of Art:
  - *Displace* – an inflatable cube reacting to concentrations of people within a particular space – designed to prevent over-crowding.
  - *Beam Me Up Scotty* – a cutting-edge electronic guide allowing visitors to a museum/gallery to extract information from exhibits by literally shining a light at them.
  - *Pavlov's Box* – a human experiment exploring how people move in public spaces with an interactive walk-through experience.
  - *3'20"* – a spectacular, collaborative experience which allows people to download digital information to create their own 3-D visual and sonic display.
  - *Navigation* – a system for showing the concentration of people visiting different areas of a museum, giving people the chance to decide to go to areas which are either busy or quiet.
- Winning entries were exhibited at the Royal College of Art, with a major launch event attended by Gestetner's commercial targets and media.
- Corporate hospitality for select members of the media and Gestetner's key customers was also organized, combining a private viewing of the Gestetner Digital Art Experience with an evening of *Tosca* at the Royal Albert Hall, adjacent to the Royal College of Art.

Evaluation

- The Gestetner Digital Art Experience was launched at the London Science Museum in October 1998, and the winning works of digital art exhibited at the Royal College of Art in February 1999. Both had a significant immediate impact on a wide variety of quality, focused media (see Table 6.2), and in customer and potential customer responses to Gestetner salespeople's approaches, and orders.

Table 6.2   *Broadcast publicity*

Broadcast	Audience	National press	Circulation
BBC 1's *Tomorrow's World*	6,000,000	*The Times* (× 2)	760,400
BBC1's *Blue Peter*	3,700,000	*The Guardian – Online*	391,238
BBC News 24	–	*The Independent – Network*	220,968
Sky Television's *Blue Screen*	77,000	*The Daily Express*	1,146,000
BBC *Radio 5 Live*	715,000	*Evening Standard*	453,600
LBC's *Steve Allen Show*	36,000		

- As well as 19 items of coverage in the trade and specialist media, the Gestetner Digital Wave also appeared on four Internet Web sites, including the *Tomorrow's World*, *Blue Peter* and *Evening Standard* Web sites.

Commercial targets

- An important part of the programme evaluation was measurement of the number of times Gestetner reached their key audience of 10,000 commercial targets via the Gestetner Digital Art Experience. The campaign succeeded in achieving repeated contact with this important group through a number of 'hits', including:
  - invitation to the launch event;
  - invitation to the exhibition;

- mailing of a Gestetner Digital Wave postcard to highlight coverage on *Tomorrow's World*;
- attendance at the launch event and exhibition;
- mailing of two issues of Gestetner's newsletter, 'Insight', focusing on the initiative;
- a Gestetner Digital Wave Christmas card;
- media coverage.

● During the period of the campaign, sales of Gestetner products have increased by 25 per cent, the largest-ever increase in the company's UK business.

Client satisfaction

Nigel Palmer, Managing Director of Gestetner, commented:

The aim of our sponsorship of the Gestetner Digital Art Experience was to reinforce our position at the leading edge of digital technology, and to demonstrate how this technology is transforming the face of the workplace as well as the art world.

We are delighted with the success of the campaign, which has provided us with a number of opportunities for direct contact with our existing and potential customers, a high level of quality media exposure, and an environment in which we have been able to dramatically increase sales.

The Communication Group has devised and delivered an outstandingly creative project, which was well managed, brilliantly communicated, and achieved all our objectives.

References

Baskin, O, Aronoff, C and Lattimore, D (1997) *Public Relations*, 4th edn, Brown & Benchmark

Bennett, R (1996) *Corporate Strategy & Business Planning*, Pitman

Bernstein, D (1991) *Company Image and Reality*, Cassell Educational Limited

Boorstin, D (1963) *The Image or What Happened to the American Dream*, Penguin Books

Boulding, E (1956) *The Image*, The University of Michigan Press

Brooking, A (1996) *Intellectual Capital/Core asset for the third millennium enterprise*, Thompson Business

Broom, G M and Dozier, D M (eds) (1990) *Using Research in Public Relations*, Prentice Hall

Brouthers, K D (1995) Strategic alliances: choose your partners, *Long Range Planning*, **28** (3), pp 18–25

Chesborough, H W and Teece, D J (1996) When is virtual virtuous: organizing for innovation, *Harvard Business Review*, January–February

Christians, C and Traeber, M (1997) *Communication Ethics and Universal Values*, Sage

Christopher, M, Payne, A and Ballantyne, D (1994) *Relationship Marketing*, Butterworth-Heinemann

Cravens, D W (1994) *Strategic Marketing*, 4th edn, Irwin

Crossman, A and McIlwee, T (1995) *Signalling Discontent: A study of the 1994 signal workers' dispute*, Thames Valley University School of Management, Thames Valley.

Dowling, C (1993) Developing your company image into a corporate asset, *Long Range Planning*, **26**, pp 101–9

Ehling, W P (1985) Application of decision theory in the construction of a theory of public relations management, II, *Public Relations Research and Education*, **2** (1), pp 4–22 in Broom, G M and Dozier, D M (eds) *Using Research in Public Relations*, Prentice Hall

Engler, P (1992) Building transnational alliances to create competitive advantage, *Long Range Planning*, **25** (1)

Ewing, M T, Caruana, A and Loy, E R (1999) Corporate reputation and perceived risk in professional engineering services, *Corporate Communication International Journal*, **4** (3), pp 121–8

Fryxell, G E and Wang, J (1994) The Fortune's Corporate Reputation Index: Reputation of what?', *Journal of Management*, **20** (1), pp 1–14

Gorb, P (1992) The psychology of corporate identity', *European Management Journal*, **10**, p 310

Grant, A W H and Schlesinger, L A (1995) Realize your customer's full profit potential, *Harvard Business Review*, September–October, pp 59–72

Gregerson, H B, Morrison, A J and Black, J S (1997) in *Frontline 21*, International Public Relations Association

Grunig, J E (ed) (1992) *Excellence in Public Relations and Communication Management*, Lawrence Erlbaum Associates

Grunig, J E and Hunt, T (1984) *Managing Public Relations*, Holt, Rinehart & Winston, Inc.

Gugler, P (1992) Building transnational alliances to create competitive advantage, *Long Range Planning*, **25** (1), pp 90–99

Guiltinan, J P and Paul, G W (1994) *Marketing Management: Strategies and programmes*, 5th edn, McGraw-Hill

Houlden, B (1988) The corporate conscience, *Management Today*, August

Ind, N (1997) *The Corporate Brand*, Macmillan Business Press Ltd

Jefkins, F (1993) *Planned Press and Public Relations*, Blackie Academic and Professional

Jobber, D (1995) *Principles and Practice of Marketing*, McGraw-Hill

Johnson, G and Scholes, K (1984) diagram in Oliver, S (1997) *Corporate Communication*, p 159, Kogan Page

Johnson, G and Scholes, K (1993) *Exploring Corporate Strategy*, Prentice Hall

Jolly, V (1996) Global strategies in the 1990s, *Mastering Management Series* no 5, Financial Times

Kirban, L and Jackson, B C (1990) Using research to plan programmes, Chapter 2 in Broom, G M and Dozier, D M (eds) *Using Research in Public Relations*, Prentice Hall

Kotler, P (1988) *Marketing Management: Analysis, Planning, Implementation and Control*, Prentice Hall International

Kotler, P (1994) *Marketing Management: Analysis, Planning, Implementation and Control*, 8th edn, Prentice Hall

Kotler, P, Armstrong, G, Saunders, J and Wong, V (1999) *Principles of Marketing*, 2nd European edition, Prentice Hall Inc

Lynch, K (1991) *The Image of the City*, The MIT Press

Maathuis, O J M (1993) *Corporate Image, Performance and Communication*, Eburon, Delft

Mackiewicz, A (1993) *Guide to Building a Global Image*, McGraw-Hill

Macrae, C (1991) *World Class Brands*, Addison-Wesley

Mayer, M (1961) *Maddison Avenue*, Penguin

McMaster (1996) Foresight: Exploring the structure of the future, *Long-Range Planning*, **29** (2), pp 149–55

McQuail, D (1994) *Mass Communication Theory*, Sage

Mintzberg, H (1994) *The Rise and Fall of Strategic Planning*, Prentice Hall

Newman, W (1956) Basic objectives which shape the character of a company, *The Journal of Business*, **26**, p 211

O'Sullivan, T, Hartley, J, Saunders, D, Montgomery, M and Fiske, J (1994) *Key Concepts in Communication and Cultural Studies*, Routledge

Oliver, S (1997) *Corporate Communication: Principles, techniques and strategies*, Kogan Page

Petrash, G (1996) Dow's journey to a knowledge value management culture, *European Management Journal*, **14** (4), pp 365–73

Porter, M (1985) *Competitive Advantage*, Free Press, New York

Quinn *et al* (1996) Managing professional intellect: making the most of the best, *Harvard Business Review*, March–April, pp 71–80

Reich, R B (1990) Who is us?, *Harvard Business Review*, January–February, in Ohmae, K (ed) (1995)

Rogers, C (1993) *Theory of Personality & Behaviour*

Singer, P (1993) *Practical Ethics*, Cambridge University Press

Smith, A and O'Neill, G (1997) Seamless marketing communications, in *CBI Corporate Communication Handbook*, Kogan Page

Stacey, R D (1993) *Strategic Management and Organizational Dynamics*, Pitman

Stacey, R R (1991) *The Chaos Frontier: Creative strategic control for business*, Butterworth-Heinemann, Oxford

Stanley, J (1991) Market communications: How Marks and Spencer does it, *European Management Journal*, **9**, pp 329–33

Stuart, H (1999) Towards a definitive model of the corporate identity management, *Corporate Communication International Journal*, **4** (4), pp 200–07

Thompson, J L (1995) *Strategy in Action*, Chapman & Hall

Van Riel, C B M (1995) *Principles of Corporate Communication*, Prentice Hall

White, J and Dozier, D M (1992) Public relations and management decision-making, in Grunig (1992)

Index

References in italic indicate figures or tables